MD Expertise comptable
COLLECTION

DCG 12

Anglais appliqué aux affaires

Préparation à l'épreuve

2e édition

Sous la direction d'Alain Burlaud
Odile Marie
Roseline Leroux
Christine Britton

Sup'FOUCHER

ISBN 978-2-216-11326-2

Sommaire

PARTIE 1

Thèmes et méthodologie

PARTIE 2

Corrigés des exercices

PARTIE 3

Sujets corrigés

Annexes

PARTIE 1

Thèmes et méthodologie

FICHE 1

La montée en puissance des pays asiatiques

1 Ground work

The Emergence of Asian Countries

Emerging markets are nations with social or business activity in the process of rapid growth and industrialization. Currently, there are 28 emerging markets in the world, with the economies of China and India considered to be by far the two largest. The ASEAN–China Free Trade Area, launched on January 1, 2010, is the largest regional emerging market in the world. These countries do not share any common agenda, but they are enjoying an increasing role in the world economy.

Japan's economic success, has been attributed to the existence of unique harmonious labour-management relations. From the 1960s to the 1980s, overall real economic growth has been called a "Japanese miracle": a 10% average in the 1960s, a 5% average in the 1970s and a 4% average in the 1980s. Growth slowed markedly in the 1990s during what the Japanese call the "Lost Decade", largely because of the after-effects of Japanese asset price bubble (1) and domestic policies intended to wring speculative excesses from the stock and real estate markets. Government efforts to revive economic growth met with little success and were further hampered (2) by the global slowdown in 2000. The economy showed strong signs of recovery after 2005. GDP growth for that year was 2.8%. As of (3) 2009, Japan is the second largest economy in the world, after the United States, at around $5 billion in terms of nominal GDP. Japan's public debt is 192 percent of its annual gross domestic product, Banking, insurance, real estate (4), retailing, transportation, telecommunications and construction are all major industries. Japan has a large industrial capacity and is home to some of the largest, leading and most technologically advanced producers of motor vehicles, electronic equipment, machine tools, steel and nonferrous metals, ships, chemicals, textiles and processed foods. The service sector accounts for three quarters of the gross domestic product.

The **Four Asian Tigers** or **Asian Tigers** are the highly developed economies of: Hong Kong, Singapore, South Korea and Taiwan. These regions were the first newly industrialized countries, noted for maintaining exceptionally high growth rates and rapid industrialization between the early 1960s and 1990s. In the 21st century, all four regions have since graduated (5) into advanced economies and high-income economies. These regions are still the world's fastest growing industrialized economies. All four Asian Tigers have a highly educated and skilled (6) workforce and have specialized in areas where they had a competitive advantage (7). They singled out (8) education as a means of improving productivity; these territories focused on improving the education system at all levels. For example, Hong Kong and Singapore became world leading international financial centres, while South Korea and Taiwan became world leaders in information technology. Their economic success stories became known as the Miracle on the Han River and the Taiwan Miracle and have served as role models for many developing countries.

China is the world's second-largest economy and its demand is playing an important role in pulling the recovery (9) in a number of economies. China's amazing growth performance has held up remarkably well. Despite many achievements (10), notably rapid improvements in living standards (11), much remains to be done.

China has become the world's largest steel (12) and car maker and a huge car market.

Ongoing (13) efforts are required to continue the process of rebalancing growth away from a reliance (14) on exports to reduce the very high national saving rate. This will help foster (15) higher consumption, further boost living standards and ensure durable growth over the longer term. In 2010, real GDP growth is 10.1%.

China's exceptional economic ascent (16) over the five years to 2008 primarily reflects huge capital investment. In contrast, labour force growth has been fairly subdued, partly due to the one-child policy. This reflects the re-allocation (17) of labour away from agriculture towards services and manufacturing.

In recent years efforts have been made to ensure that by the age of 15, all children have had 9 years of primary and junior high school education. Universities made significant investments to triple the number of new entrants into tertiary education.

India (nicknamed «the elephant»). In 2009, India's nominal GDP stood at $1.243 billion, which makes it the eleventh-largest economy in the world, corresponding to a per capita income of US$3,100. The country ranks 139th in nominal GDP per capita. With an average annual GDP growth rate of 5.8% for the past two decades, the economy is among the fastest growing in the world.

India has the world's second largest labour force, with 516.3 million people. In terms of output, the agricultural sector accounts for 28% of GDP; the service and industrial sectors make up 54% and 18% respectively. Major industries include textiles, chemicals, food processing (18), steel, transport equipment, cement, mining, petroleum, machinery, software. In 2008, India's share of world trade was about 1.68%. Major exports include petroleum products, textile goods, gems (19) and jewelry, software, engineering goods, chemicals, and leather (20) manufactures. Major imports include crude oil, machinery, gems, fertilizer (21), chemicals.

Seven of the world's top 15 technology outsourcing (22) companies are based in India and the country is viewed as the second most favourable outsourcing destination after the United States. Despite India's impressive economic growth over recent decades, it still contains the largest concentration of poor people in the world. Although the Indian economy has grown steadily over the last two decades, India will remain a low-income country for several decades, with per capita incomes well below its other BRIC peers (23).

1. *The Japanese asset price bubble* was an economic bubble in Japan from 1986 to 1991, in which real estate and stock prices greatly inflated. The bubble's collapse lasted for more than a decade with stock prices bottoming in 2003, until hitting an even lower low amidst the current global crisis in 2008.
2. *to hamper* : gêner
3. *as of* : à partir de
4. *real estate* : immobilier
5. *to graduate* : passer de ... à ...
6. *skilled* : qualifié
7. *competitive advantage* : avantage concurrentiel
8. *to single out* : sélectionner
9. *recovery* : reprise
10. *achievements* : exploits, réussites
11. *living standards* : niveau de vie

12. *steel* : acier
13. *ongoing* : en cours
14. *reliance* : dépendance
15. *to foster* : favoriser, encourager
16. *ascent* : rise
17. *re-allocation* : redistribution, réaffectation
18. *food processing* : industrie alimentaire
19. *gems* : gemmes, pierres précieuses
20. *leather* : cuir
21. *fertilizer* : engrais
22. *outsourcing* : délocalisation, externalisation
23. *peer* : homologue

The term "rapidly developing economies" is being used to denote emerging markets such as The United Arab Emirates, Chile and Malaysia that are undergoing rapid growth.
In recent years, new terms have emerged to describe the largest developing countries such as BRIC that stands for Brazil, China, India and Russia, along with BRICS (BRIC + South Africa), BRICM (BRIC + Mexico) and BRICK (BRIC + South Korea).
The Big Emerging Market (BEM) economies are Brazil, China, Pakistan, Egypt, India, Indonesia, Mexico, Philippines, Poland, Russia, South Africa, South Korea and Turkey.

2 Zooming on

India and China: the Friendly Giants

Why can China build cities overnight while India has trouble building roads? Why does China ban free elections while Indians vote in officials with criminal records?

The economic rise of the world's two most populous countries will enrich us all, argues the Harvard professor Tarun Khanna.

These are just some of the questions the Harvard Business School professor Tarun Khanna takes up in his book, Billions of Entrepreneurs: How China and India Are Reshaping Their Futures and Yours.

The soft-spoken Khanna, who talked to hundreds of business people and policymakers for his book, has offered an optimistic take on the rise of India and China with their combined population of 2.4 billion. Not for him the scaremongering found among commentators such as the CNN anchor Lou Dobbs, who warns about the loss of American jobs to China, as well as defective Chinese products.

In a sense the growing economic might of these two Asian giants – although some would say with feet of clay – is a case of back to the future. In the 1800s as much as 50% of world GDP was accounted for by China and India. Khanna is pragmatic about both countries: they have achieved economic success through very different methods and he lays out the strengths and weaknesses of the two "petri dishes" of economic development.

As befitting a Harvard business professor, Khanna is a market liberal. But he acknowledges the effectiveness of China's top-down approach, a capitalism (of sorts) imposed from above that has lifted millions out of poverty, while creating new cities that rival New York and London. Yet he takes note of the downside; the lack of clear property rights and democratic freedoms that could hinder further economic progress.

India's economic model is a messier affair. In a sometimes raucous democracy, where the voters regularly vote in MPs with criminal records, the task of central government, more often than not, is to get out of the way and let the private sector drive growth and create jobs. India can't build gleaming cities overnight because the government is too weak to bulldoze slums to make room for skyscrapers.

China's approach to economic development – centred on manufacturing and big infrastructure projects, from dams to rail – and to foreign policy typifies "hard power". India, with its software industry and Bollywood films, represents "soft power".

Khanna coins the term "mutualism" to describe the synthesis of these two economic approaches that will benefit not just China and India but the rest of the world. He cites the case of GE Healthcare, the health arm of the US corporate giant General Electric. GE was unique because it succeeded both in China and India and its operations are more than a sum of its parts.

GE Healthcare took the best from both countries to develop its medical equipment and has opened research and development centres in Shanghai and Bangalore. Since writing the book, Khanna says he has discovered hundreds more examples of cross-fertilisation.

"The ability to set up parallel groups of highly skilled engineering talent in both countries is invaluable," a GE executive told Khanna. "It raises the efficiency of product development and fits in with a competitive culture within GE."

Not all commentators buy this "rosy scenario". In his book, Rivals: How the Power Struggle Between China, India and Japan Will Shape Our Next Decade, Bill Emmott, the former editor-in-chief of the Economist, offers a bleaker vision of the rise of Asia.

"An array of disputes, historical bitternesses and regional flashpoints weigh down on all three countries. Conflict is not inevitable but nor is it inconceivable. If it were to occur – over Taiwan, say, or the Korean peninsula or Tibet or Pakistan – it would not simply be an intra-Asian affair. The outside world would be drawn in."

Khanna acknowledges the existence of such security concerns, but thinks it bad social science to extrapolate from the past 40 years of tension between India and China.

"It is equally plausible to see the rise of economic development between two friendly countries," says Khanna, a self-avowed optimist who thinks increased human contact between India and China can only be positive. "There is nothing to suggest hostility between India and China beyond the occasional sabre-rattling over border disputes."

guardian.co.uk, April 25th, 2008, by Mark Tran

The power to disrupt

Business innovations from emerging markets will change the rich world too

[...] These days the third world is known as the emerging markets, the Che Guevara T-shirts are made in China and the wretched of the earth are enjoying growth rates that are the envy of the former colonial powers. Moreover, these emerging markets are likely to shake things up not only in their own backyards but in rich countries too. Clayton Christensen, of the Harvard Business School, has coined the term "disruptive innovation" for new products that slash prices and new processes that radically change the way they are made and delivered. Today many of these disruptive innovations hail from the emerging markets. They will make a bigger difference to life in the West than lean production, the previous great disruptive management innovation from the East.

There are four reasons why things will move faster and further this time. The first is that the markets for corporate control and for senior managerial talent are much more liquid than they were 20 years ago. The great Japanese and South Korean giants grew organically, whereas emerging-market champions are keen on mergers and acquisitions. They have access to highly developed capital markets, both public and private, and to armies of experienced investment bankers and consultants. In 2007, before the crisis struck, Chinese companies did $30 billion-worth of outbound deals, 60% more than the previous year and $5 billion more than inbound deals. The figure for Indian companies was $35 billion, five times more than the previous year and $10 billion more than inbound deals. The gold rush continues. This year has already produced two mega-bids by Indian giants: Bharti Airtel's for Zain and Reliance's for LyondellBasell.

The second factor is the sheer size of the emerging markets. The Japanese export machine was powered by just a few engines, notably cars and electronics. By contrast, the emerging-market export machine has engines in almost every industry. ArcelorMittal is the world's biggest steel company. Infosys and TCS are among the world's biggest IT companies. Haier is the fourth-largest manufacturer of home appliances. ZTE, which started foreign operations only in 1997, looks set to become one of the world's top five mobile-handset maker. Just a decade ago not a single emerging-market company could be considered world-class. Today such companies are among the world's leaders in 25 big industries, according to the Boston Consulting Group.

The third reason to expect a big impact is the emphasis on volume. Emerging-market companies are obsessed by finding new markets to make up for their slim profit margins. Indian and Chinese mobile-phone companies have been adding 8m-10m new subscribers a month for the past few years. Emerging-world giants such as Infosys and ZTE have been growing at more than 40% a year.

Fourth, the West's best companies have grasped the potential of emerging markets. Henry Ford II, who ran the Ford Motor Company for decades after the Second World War, continued into the 1980s to dismiss Japanese cars as "those little shitboxes". By contrast, the best Western companies are now looking to emerging markets as sources of innovation and growth. Cisco expects 20% of its best people to work in its "Cisco East" centre in the future. Britain's Prudential, a financial-services company, has recently bid $35.5 billion for the Asian assets of American International Group. If the bid goes through, the company will be earning more than half its overall profits from Asia.

The West is ripe for frugal innovation. Western consumers and governments have been on a debt-fuelled spending spree for many years. American household debt rose from 65% of GDP in the mid-1990s to 95% in 2009. The American government was cutting taxes and raising public spending even before the recession struck. The British government increased public spending from 35% of GDP in 2000-01 to 43% in 2009-10.

Look at my new hair shirt

Now the age of profligacy is giving way to an age of austerity. Governments are having to put their fiscal houses in order and consumers are cutting back on their spending, worried about unemployment and shrinking wealth (American household wealth dropped by 22% between 2007 and 2009). An annual survey of consumer spending by Booz & Company suggests that two-thirds of Americans are trading down and buying cheaper items. Andy Bond, the boss of Asda, a British retailer, says the frivolous is now unacceptable and the frugal is "cool".

But these spending cuts will inevitably dampen growth in the West, creating yet more demand for frugality. Historically, big financial crises have been followed by long periods of slow growth and economic malaise, and the recent crisis has been bigger than most. Olivier Blanchard, the IMF's chief economist, predicts that painful retrenchment in Europe could last for 20 years.

Moreover, the need for such retrenchment comes at a time when demand for welfare services is rising as the baby-boomers start to retire and medical innovations push up health-care costs. By 2050 one in three people across the rich world will be drawing a pension. America's Congressional Budget Office predicts that spending on entitlements will grow from 10% of GDP today to 16% in 2035. Many European countries, particularly in the south, will come under even greater pressure. The search for cutbacks in public spending will become ever more urgent. According to Thomson Reuters, America's health-care system wastes $600 billion-850 billion every year because of inefficient administration, unnecessary treatment and litigation costs. (On the other hand it has proved to be a huge job-creation machine.)

Dr Shetty first started thinking about the dismal management of health care when, as a trainee doctor at Guy's hospital in London, he had to spend hours sitting around doing nothing. Most Western bureaucrats try to deal with such problems with successive rounds of cost-cutting. But the experience of the emerging markets suggests that "cost innovation"—redesigning both products and processes from scratch to take out costs—is a much more productive strategy.

A growing number of Western company bosses have become aware of the potential for such innovations to change the way business is done in the West. Carlos Ghosn of Renault has praised India's frugal innovation. Jeff Immelt of GE has backed the idea that his company should disrupt itself with cheap products from India and China. When Arun Sarin was boss of Vodafone, he sent his top executives to India to learn about its low-cost business model.

Shifting the centre of gravity

The same message can be heard from management gurus. Peter Williamson, of the Judge Business School at the University of Cambridge, regards emerging markets as repositories of "value-for-money strategies for recessionary times". John Hagel and John Seely Brown have even predicted "blowback" from emerging-world innovations: the Western companies that exported capitalism to developing countries in the first place may soon find themselves humbled by more innovative companies from that part of the world.

Frugal innovation is already beginning to make itself felt in the West, particularly in health care. GE's cheap ultrasound device, originally developed for the Chinese market, has become the basis of a global business, with eager customers in the developed as well as the developing world. This year 6m Americans are expected to travel to developing countries such as India in search of affordable health care, up from 750,000 in 2007. At the same time Dr Shetty is building a 2,000-bed hospital in the Cayman Islands, a short flight from Miami, where he will offer surgery at half the price charged by American hospitals.

But the trend is apparent in consumer goods too. Haier has become the market leader in the West for cheap fridges. Most Western carmakers are producing small, inexpensive vehicles that have been influenced by the Nano. Mahindra & Mahindra's nifty little tractors are popular with hobby farmers and gardeners in America.

Westerners have long been less enthusiastic about globalisation than people in emerging markets. According to the 2009 Pew Global Attitudes Project, only 65% of Americans think that external trade and business ties are good for their country, compared with more than 90% of Indians and Chinese. Hostility to globalisation in the developed world is likely to grow as emerging giants disrupt one product market after another. Yet such disruption will bring benefits as well as problems for rich countries. Re-engineered medical devices could slash health-care costs without reducing the quality of care. Compact cars will allow people to keep driving but cause less damage to the environment.

The developed world still has some powerful weapons in its arsenal. The average Western company is much better managed than the average emerging-world company (see chart 6): for every Infosys and Haier there are plenty of poorly managed and uncompetitive firms in developing countries. America in particular is remarkably good at encouraging entrepreneurial start-ups and allowing them to grow. Michael Gibbert, of Italy's Bocconi University, notes that the West also has a long tradition of inventiveness in hard times, demonstrated during the Second World War. Mr Williamson points out that Western companies such as Wal-Mart are already making a success of value-for-money strategies. And some of the most articulate promoters of reverse engineering and frugal innovation from emerging countries run Western companies or teach in Western business schools.

Even so, the new management paradigm now taking shape in the emerging world has big implications for the global balance of power. The world's creative energy is shifting to the developing countries, which are becoming innovators in their own right rather than just talented imitators. A growing number of the world's business innovations will in future come not from "the West" but "the rest".

Anand Mahindra, vice-chairman of the eponymous family firm, says that these days when Indians go to bed at night their dreams about their country's future "are not just colourful but steroidal". His compatriots are at last beginning to believe that "the sandcastles we build in our minds are not going to be simply washed away by the morning tide." The same is true across the emerging world, whose "sandcastles" are now being built on the solid foundations of business innovation. They will endure, changing not just emerging markets but the rest of the world as well.

The Economist, April 15th, 2010

ODI : emerging countries increasingly affect the growth prospects of poorer ones

Just about every day some piece of news comes along that highlights how the balance of the world economy shifts a little further – away from the developed world (basically North America, Western Europe, Japan and Australasia) and towards the emerging world. That is an even swifter shift than that envisaged by Goldman Sachs in its renowned report on the BRICs. If the NIESR proves right, the defining moment of the decade we have just entered will be the US ceding its position as the world's largest economy, a place it has held for more than a century. When that happens it changes everything.

The process is sometimes direct (through aid, trade, remittances, investment) and sometimes

indirect (through commodity prices or competition in third markets, for instance).
The crisis has forced the move from the G-7 to the G-20 and led to the recognition of the growth of the BRICs. For the first time the once-poor countries were sitting at the table as equal partners and making their weight felt in international negotiations.
This month, Sri Lanka got $290m from China for a new international airport and $67m from India to upgrade its railways. As poor countries emerge from recession and the rich world flounders, big middle-income countries see a once-in-a-generation chance to win friends and influence people.
China is now the largest donor to Cambodia and Sri Lanka. It has a huge list of pledges to Africa. In November the Prime Minister, Wen Jiabao, promised $10 billion of cheap loans over three years. China has also offered debt forgiveness, new hospitals, professional training for 15,000 Africans and a doubling of aid between 2006 and 2009.
Similarly for trade: poor-country exports to rich countries have fallen much faster (down by 17% in 2008-09) than those to emerging markets (down by only 7%). In three-quarters of the poor countries that the ODI looked at, middle-income countries have increased their share of trade.
Trade and foreign direct investment (FDI) from the West are already falling and the middle-income countries are taking up the slack. While total FDI in Africa fell by about a third between 2008 and 2009, the flow from China soared by 80%. Brazil says it has invested $10 billion on the continent since 2003. Since 2009, the BRICs' deals in Africa have become a flood.
Deep down most of us can't quite believe it will happen, perhaps because it forces us to rethink all our embedded ideas about global leadership, the importance of the North American/European consensus on democracy, the market economy, the rule of law and so on. But the evidence of the shift of power becomes harder and harder to deny.

Adapted from http://www.odi.org/uk

Useful language

to abide by : respecter
allegations : accusations
blowback : retour de souffle, retour de flamme
border : frontière
bribes : des pots-de-vin
buyout : un rachat d'entreprise
to compete : concurrencer
cutback : réduction
developing countries : pays envoie de développement
to disrupt : déranger, interrompre
entitlements : droits (à la retraite)
to flounder : patauger
forecasts : les prévisions
foreign policy : la politique étrangère
foreign trade : le commerce extérieur
free flow : la liberté de circulation
to fund : financer
global corporation : une multinationale
gold rush : la ruée vers l'or
growth : la croissance

hail from : en provenance de
to improve the welfare of workers : améliorer les conditions de vie des travailleurs
to invest abroad : investir a l'étranger
labour market : le marché du travail
to liberalize : libéraliser
low wages : bas salaires
manpower : la main-d'œuvre
mega bid : offre énorme
merger : fusion
monopoly : le monopole
moonlighting : travail au noir
to outsource/ delocalise : délocaliser
outsourcing : la délocalisation
policy : une politique
profligacy : prodigalité
relocation : la délocalisation
retrenchment : restrictions de dépenses
to settle : s'implanter
start-up : création d'entreprise
subsidiary : une filiale
supply and demand : l'offre et la demande
sweatshop : un atelier (où les ouvriers sont exploités)
the charter of human rights : la charte des droits fondamentaux
the economics situation : la conjoncture
the rule of law : l'autorité de la loi
the Third World : le tiers monde
ties : liens
to trade down : changer pour quelque chose de meilleur marché
to treat fairly/unfairly : traiter équitablement ou injustement
unfair competition : concurrence déloyale
welfare state : état providence
wretched of the earth : les déshérités de la terre
ODI : The Overseas Development Institute, a British think-tank. [«udi:Ai]
BRICs : The acronym was coined to bring together the four largest emerging economies of Brazil (187m people), Russia (140m), India (1.1bn), and China (1.3 billion). A BRIC is a country from the emerging world that is already three percent of global GDP (china is the only one), or has a realistic chance of becoming three percent GDP.
FDI : Foreign Direct Investment [efdi:Ai]
NIESR : The National Institute of Economic and Social Research, Britain's longest-established independent institute of economic and social research
take up the slack : to do or provide something that another organisation is no longer doing or providing (relancer)
upgrade : improve, make more efficient – downgrade: be given less importance than before

3 Comprehension of documents

Exercice 1.1

Donnez le mot correspondant à la définition.

1. accusations
2. a place where workers are exploited
3. another word for the developing world
4. to respect laws
5. when goods can circulate freely

Exercice 1.2

Traduisez en français.

1. The economic rise of the world's two most populous countries will enrich us all, argues the Harvard professor Tarun Khanna.
2. The soft-spoken Khanna, who talked to hundreds of business people and policymakers for his book, has offered an optimistic take on the rise of India and China with their combined population of 2.4 billion.
3. In a sometimes raucous democracy, where the voters regularly vote in MPs with criminal records, the task of central government, more often than not, is to get out of the way and let the private sector drive growth and create jobs.
4. China's approach to economic development – centred on manufacturing and big infrastructure projects, from dams to rail – and to foreign policy typifies "hard power".
5. If it were to occur – over Taiwan, say, or the Korean peninsula or Tibet or Pakistan – it would not simply be an intra-Asian affair. The outside world would be drawn in.

Exercice 1.3

En utilisant les documents *The power to disrupt* et *ODI: emerging countries increasingly affect the growth prospects of poorer ones*, rédigez un résumé de 300 mots en anglais qui mettra en lumière les changements dus aux pays émergents suite à la crise économique actuelle ; aussi bien en occident que dans les pays en voie de développement.

FICHE 2

Méthode
Compréhension de l'écrit

La compréhension de texte est souvent le point de départ d'autres types d'exercices comme la lecture d'un article, afin d'en faire le résumé ou le commentaire, ou la synthèse (lorsque celui-ci fait partie d'un ensemble de documents). Il faut donc s'entraîner régulièrement à la lecture et à la compréhension de textes. Vous trouverez quelques pistes qui vous aideront à comprendre un texte, puis à l'analyser.

1 La nature du document

Déterminez tout d'abord précisément la nature du document à étudier (article de journal, de magazine, page de site web...).

Identifiez ensuite la source, le nom de l'auteur et la date de publication : ces éléments peuvent vous fournir des indices importants. Vous pouvez compléter le tableau suivant (l'analyse donnée à titre d'exemple porte sur le document de la Fiche 1 ***India and China: the Friendly Giants***).

Type of document	*article from a website*
Source	*guardian.co.uk*
Author	*Mark Tran*
Date	*25th April 2008*

2 Le titre et les éléments paratextuels

Lisez attentivement le titre. S'il y a un sous-titre, lisez le également très attentivement, celui-ci vous apportera sans doute des indications supplémentaires importantes sur le thème traité dans l'article. Faites de même avec le premier paragraphe qui comporte souvent l'essentiel des informations.

Observez aussi tous les éléments tels que photos ou graphiques lorsqu'il y en a.

Title	*India and China : the Friendly Giants*
Subtitle	*Why can China build cities overnight while India has trouble building roads? Why does China ban free elections while Indians vote in officials with criminal records?*
Topic	*The similarities and the differences between two Asian countries/India and China (their advantages and their drawbacks as far as the economy is concerned)*

3 La compréhension globale

La première lecture (ou les premières lectures) devrait vous permettre de répondre aux questions en « Wh ».

Who	*(a book by) Tarun Khanna*
What	*economic rise*
Where	*India and China*
When	*nowadays (verbs in the present tense mainly) and in the future*
Why	

4 La recherche du vocabulaire inconnu

Ne vous laissez pas impressionner par le vocabulaire inconnu. Essayez de repérer les mots essentiels à la compréhension et d'en inférer le sens.

A. Les mots transparents

Les mots transparents vous permettent de vous repérer dans le texte. Ne les négligez pas mais faites attention aux faux amis (***deceptive words*** ou ***false cognates*** en anglais).

Exercice 2.1

Trouvez un faux ami dans le texte du document *India and China: the Friendly Giants* de la Fiche 1.

B. Les mots dérivés (derived words)

Certains mots vous semblent inconnus mais vous pouvez cependant en reconnaître une partie (la base). Ce sont les mots dérivés. Voici des exemples de mots dérivés :

Mot	Base	Préfixe	Suffixe	Nature	Traduction
weaknesses	weak (adj.)	Ø	**ness/es**	plural noun	faibl**esses**
acknowledge	to know	ac	ledge	verb	reconnaître

Exercice 2.2

Trouvez d'autres mots dérivés dans le texte du document *India and China: the Friendly Giants*. Vous pouvez recopier et remplir une grille sur le modèle ci-dessus.

C. Les mots composés (compound words)

D'autres mots sont composés de deux parties qui donnent naissance à de nouveaux mots. Ce sont les mots composés. Voici des exemples de mots composés :

Mot	Composition	Nature	Traduction
policy maker	policy + to make + suffix "er"	noun	stratège
soft spoken	adjective + past participle	adjective	à la voix douce, calme

Exercice 2.3

Trouvez d'autres mots composés dans le texte du document *India and China: the Friendly Giants*. Vous pouvez recopier et remplir une grille sur le modèle ci-dessus.

D. Le contexte

Le contexte peut vous permettre d'éclaircir le sens de certains mots qui vous sont inconnus. Observez bien les phrases et essayez de déduire le sens de ces mots. Par exemple :

Mot	Contexte ou mots connus	Traduction
to take up	(questions) he takes up	se poser des questions, les aborder
scaremongering	scare/scary	alarmisme
loss	to lose/lost	la perte

Exercice 2.4

En vous appuyant sur le contexte du texte *India and China: the Friendly Giants*, essayez de deviner le sens de *defective*, *befitting*, *lifted*, *hinder*, *slums*.

E. Les mots de liaison (link-words) et les prépositions (prepositions)

D'autres mots peuvent vous permettre de progresser dans la compréhension de texte : ce sont les prépositions et les mots de liaison.

Mots de liaison		Prépositions	
although	bien que	*beyond*	au-delà

Exercice 2.5

Trouvez d'autres mots de liaison et d'autres prépositions dans le texte du document *India and China: the Friendly Giants*.

F. Les pronoms relatifs (relative pronouns), adjectifs ou pronoms démonstratifs ou possessifs (possessive or demonstrative adjectives or pronouns)

Il est indispensable de savoir exactement à quoi renvoient les pronoms relatifs et les adjectifs ou pronoms possessifs afin de comprendre le sens des phrases.

Pronom ou adjectif	Représente
who	*Khanna*
their	*India and China*
that	*lack of clear property rights and democratic freedoms*

Exercice 2.6

Dans le texte du document *India and China: the Friendly Giants*, trouvez à qui, ou à quoi, les mots suivants font référence : « these », « its », « his », « who ».

G. Les verbes (leur temps, leur aspect)

Ceux-ci déterminent le moment de l'action et l'implication de l'auteur dans ce qui est écrit.

Verbe	Temps	Indication
talked	simple past	past and completed action, no link with the present
will enrich	future	it will take place in the future!
has offered	present perfect	the action is going on in the present though it began in the pats

Exercice 2.7

En lisant le texte du document *India and China: the Friendly Giants*, trouvez les temps et les indications données par les verbes suivants : ***vote***, ***were***.

H. Les auxiliaires modaux

Les auxiliaires modaux donnent une idée supplémentaire de l'implication de l'auteur. Ils permettent de déduire le jugement que celui-ci peut porter sur l'action.

Auxiliaire modal	Implication
can	ability to do something
would	conditional

Exercice 2.8

Trouvez un autre auxiliaire modal dans le texte du document *India and China: the Friendly Giants* et dites ce qu'il implique.
Connaissez-vous d'autres auxiliaires modaux ?

I. La phrase minimale (minimal sentence)

Lorsqu'une phrase est très longue, découpez-la en unités de sens. Elle deviendra alors beaucoup plus simple.

- **Exemple**
The soft-spoken Khanna, who talked to hundreds of business people and policymakers for his book, has offered an optimistic take on the rise of India and China with their combined population of 2.4 billion.
devient :
Khanna has offered an optimistic take on the rise of India and China.

Exercice 2.9

Réécrivez ces deux phrases en deux phrases minimales.

China's approach to economic development – centred on manufacturing and big infrastructure projects, from dams to rail – and to foreign policy typifies "hard power". India, with its software industry and Bollywood films, represents "soft power".

Exercice 2.10

Répondez aux questions concernant le texte du document *India and China: the Friendly Giants*.

1. What book is referred to in this article? Who wrote it? What ideas does it defend?
2. Which countries are mentioned? What do you learn about them?
3. What are their advantages and their drawbacks?
4. Does everybody share Tarun Khanna's opinion? Explain.

FICHE 3

La globalisation des marchés

1 Ground work

Globalised Markets

Buying foreign goods is not a new thing: in the Middle Ages, ships sailed (1) East to bring back spices and other luxuries. Nowadays the range (2) of foreign products available to us is enormous. It is no longer usual for manufactured products to be made near the place of purchase (3). Most clothes, textiles and household goods (4) bought in Europe are made elsewhere.

▸ Reasons for the rapid rise in global markets

- Multinational corporations have outlets (5) in different countries.
- Transport has increased in efficiency and decreased in cost. Containers can be offloaded (6) quickly in modern docks; air transport ensures fast delivery (7) of perishable goods.
- With the WTO's agreements for lower tariff barriers, trade has been liberalised.
- Information and communication technologies have grown at break-neck speed (8), enabling trans-national ordering and delivering *via* internet.

▸ The new world economy

The emerging countries, China, Brazil, and India, have taken a large share of world markets.
Consumers world-wide have a wider choice of cheaper products.
Multinational companies make profits by relocating (9) to places where production costs are cheaper.

▸ The influence of financial markets

As well as the free movement of goods, globalisation has seen the free movement of capital.
Computer-programmed (10) speculation and immediate communications increase the severity of financial crises. The subprime (11) crisis of 2007-2010 had enduring (12) devastating effects.
Instability in the world has increased, as we have recently witnessed (13) in Greece.

▸ Harmful effects

Poorer countries provide the workforce (14): workers rights, such as freedom to join a Trade Union, are not always respected; child labour (15) is frequently used.
Prosperity has not increased everywhere: a large part of the world's population has to live on 2 dollars a day while inequality between rich and poor has risen.

▸ The anti-free trade and alter-globalisation movements

Given the harmful effects on environment, health and prosperity, opposition is reflected in these movements. The "alter" movements emphasise that there are good sides to

globalisation, such as sharing of information, but wish to set up a more humane (16) and less polluting world economy.
Cultural globalisation follows in the footsteps (17) of globalised markets, and alter-globalists want to resist the all-embracing (18) influence of American media.

1. *to sail* : naviguer
2. *range* : ensemble de choix
3. *purchase* : achat
4. *household goods* : articles de ménage et électroménager
5. *outlets* : débouchés
6. *to offload* : décharger
7. *delivery* : livraison
8. *break-neck speed* : vitesse vertigineuse
9. *relocating* : delocalisation
10. *computer*-programmed : programmé sur ordinateur
11. *subprime* : achat de créances non payées et non payables
12. *enduring* : qui dure
13. *to witness* : être témoin
14. *workforce* : l'ensemble des travailleurs
15. *child labour* : travail des enfants
16. *humane* : compatissant
17. *to follow in the footsteps* : suivre exactement (la trace des pas)
18. *all-embracing* : qui englobe tout

2 Zooming on

Outsourcing Works, So India Is Exporting Jobs

MYSORE, India

Thousands of Indians report to Infosys Technologies' campus here to learn the finer points of programming. Lately, though, packs of foreigners have been roaming the manicured lawns, too. […]
Many of them are recent American college graduates, and some have even turned down job offers from coveted employers like Google. Instead, they accepted a novel assignment from Infosys, the Indian technology giant: fly here for six months of training, then return home to work in the company's American back offices.
India is outsourcing outsourcing.
One of the constants of the global economy has been companies moving their tasks – and jobs – to India. But rising wages and a stronger currency here, demands for workers who speak languages other than English, and competition from countries looking to emulate India's success as a back office – including China, Morocco and Mexico – are challenging that model.
Many executives here acknowledge that outsourcing, having rained most heavily on India, will increasingly sprinkle tasks around the globe. Or, as Ashok Vemuri, an Infosys senior vice president, put it, the future of outsourcing is "to take the work from any part of the world and do it in any part of the world." […]
Infosys is building a whole archipelago of back offices – in Mexico, the Czech Republic, Thailand and China, as well as low-cost regions of the United States.
The company seeks to become a global matchmaker for outsourcing: any time a company wants work done somewhere else, even just down the street, Infosys wants to get the call. It is a peculiar ambition for a company that symbolizes the flow of tasks from the West to India.

Most of Infosys's 75,000 employees are Indians, in India. They account for most of the company's $3.1 billion in sales in the year that ended March 31, from work for clients like Bank of America and Goldman Sachs.

"India continues to be the No. 1 location for outsourcing," S. Gopalakrishnan, the company's chief executive, said in a telephone interview [...].

The New York Times, September 25th, 2007, by Anand Giridharadas

India's Outsourcing Industry Is Facing a Labor Shortage

MUMBAI, India, Feb. 16

India's leadership in global outsourcing may be in jeopardy unless it increases its supply of skilled workers, according to executives gathered here for an industry meeting.

Experts at the meeting of Nasscom, the country's outsourcing group, said Thursday that an incipient skills shortage was the biggest threat to the industry's blazing growth.

As the meeting opened Wednesday, Pramod Bhasin, chief executive of Genpact, a back-office outsourcing company once owned by General Electric, set the tone when he said, "If the talent in India is scarce, we will go wherever the labor pool is available."

Lower-cost centers like Eastern Europe and China could become serious rivals for outsourcing business from Western multinational companies. Until now, corporations mainly looked to India to do work from customer support to writing software code to designing chips. But the supply of India's famed "skilled, low-cost, English-speaking" work force may not quite match the sizzling demand.

India's $23.4 billion outsourcing industry accounts for most of the country's software and services industry, which makes up nearly 5 percent of gross domestic product. The industry employs 1.2 million workers, has sparked a consumer revolution in India, and is accelerating at more than 30 percent a year.

On the sidelines of the Nasscom meeting, B. Ramalinga Raju, chairman of India's fourth-largest outsourcing company, Satyam Computer Services, said that India produced three million college graduates every year, including nearly 400,000 engineers. "But most of these are uncut diamonds that have to go through polishing factories, as the trade requires only polished stones," Mr. Raju said. In a country of 1.1 billion people, raw talent is plentiful, he said, but not all of it is market-ready.

Sensing the threat, government and industry are scrambling. Nasscom has begun a skill assessment and certification program for entry-level employees in back-office work; the group has plans to create such program for software services. The government has introduced computer classes in schools. Companies are working with academic institutions so that graduating students will have skills tailored to the job market. [...]

The New York Times, February 16th, 2006, by Saritha Rai

Protesters force Tata Motors to abandon a car factory in West Bengal

DELHI

EACH year India's Bengalis celebrate the goddess Durga, offering prayers before dazzling religious tableaux called *pandals*. This year Santosh Mitra square in Kolkata (formerly Calcutta) hosted an unusual example: a yellow replica of the Nano, the small car touted by Tata Motors as the world's cheapest. It stood in front of a forlorn factory (pictured), made of plywood, fibreglass and plaster, and girdled by a huge padlock and chain. Alas, the Nano will not be built in West Bengal. On October 3rd Ratan Tata, chairman of the Tata Group, said his firm would abandon its factory in the state, which has been pinned down for months in "political crossfire".

The Nano is an icon of Indian ingenuity and entrepreneurialism. Selling for just 100,000 rupees ($2,100), it seeks to reach a new class of customers through frugal engineering. But India's politicians also have a keen eye for a gap in the market. Mamata Banerjee, leader of the main opposition party in West Bengal, drummed up a campaign on behalf of farmers who opposed the project. Many had refused the compensation the state government offered when it hurriedly expropriated their land to make room for the Tata Motors plant. Whatever the justice of its cause, the campaign became shrill and intimidating. It has undone West Bengal's efforts to court industrial investment, and may have done wider damage to India's reputation. If the Tatas, one of India's most venerable business houses, cannot build a factory without political grief, why should foreign investors take the risk?

Farming accounts for less than 18% of India's output, but carries far greater political weight. The difficulty of acquiring land, which is often either treasured by farmers or hoarded by the state, has become a constraint on India's growth. Industrialists are converting over 466,000 acres into business-friendly "special economic zones". But not without fuss. In Maharashtra the government should soon release the results of a farmers' referendum on a project outside Mumbai championed by Mukesh Ambani, head of Reliance Industries, India's biggest company by market capitalisation. In Goa the government renounced all such zones amid popular concerns about the changing character of the state.

In fact, only the setbacks grab the headlines. India has enjoyed an astonishing boom in manufacturing investment, despite all these obstacles. [...]

The Economist print edition, October 9th, 2008

Useful language

abroad/overseas : à l'étranger
agreement : accord
alter-globalist : alter mondialiste
alternative : alternatif
ban : interdiction
to break into a market : faire son entrée sur un marché
bribes : pots de vin
buyout : rachat d'entreprise
to capture, corner a market : s'emparer d'un marché
a challenge : un défi
to compete with : concurrencer
controversial : sujet à controverses
controversy : polémique
developing countries : pays en voie de développement
dispute : conflit
downturn : la régression
drop, decline : baisse
economic situation : conjoncture
emerging countries : pays émergents
Fair Trade : commerce équitable
FDI (Foreign Direct Investment) : IDE (Investissements Directs à l'Étranger)
forecast : prévision
foreign trade : le commerce extérieur
free trade : le libre échange
free trade area (FTA) : zone de libre échange
free trade agreement (FTA) : accord de libre échange

to fund : financer
GDP (Gross Domestic Product) : PIB (Produit Intérieur Brut)
global : mondial
global corporation : une multinationale
globalization : la mondialisation
GNP (Gross National Product) : PNB (Produit National Brut)
grant : une subvention
guideline : directive
home trade : le commerce intérieur
IMF (International Monetary Fund) : FMI (Fonds Monétaire International)
to increase, to boost, to bolster : dynamiser, augmenter
to invest abroad : investir à l'étranger
know-how : savoir faire
lobby : un groupe de pression
market share : part de marché
monopoly : le monopole
*negotiation*négociation :
to offshore (US) : délocaliser
to outsource : délocaliser
outsourcing : la délocalisation
poverty : la pauvreté
premium price : le prix fort
profitability : la rentabilité
purchasing power/spending power : pouvoir d'achat
recovery : la reprise économique
to relocate : délocaliser
rock bottom price : prix défiant toute concurrence
slowdown : ralentissement
standard of living : le niveau de vie
subsidiary : une filiale
to subsidise : subventionner
subsidy : subvention
to support : soutenir
takeover : prise de contrôle
tariff : droits de douane
tax-free : exempt d'impôt
tax haven : paradis fiscal
trade : échanges commerciaux
unfair competition : concurrence déloyale
World Bank : Banque Mondiale
World Social Forum (WSF) : Forum Social Mondial
WTO (World Trade Organisation) : OMT (Organisation Mondiale du Commerce)
worldwide : dans le monde entier

3 Comprehension of documents

Exercice 3.1

Donnez les mots correspondant aux définitions.

1. a country where you don't pay any tax
2. a branch of a big firm
3. a person who believes there is an alternative to globalisation
4. when people don't agree, the subject is...
5. the lowest price possible on the market

Exercice 3.2

Traduisez en français.

1. Many of them are recent American college graduates, and some have even turned down job offers from coveted employers like Google.
2. Lower-cost centers like Eastern Europe and China could become serious rivals for outsourcing business from Western multinational companies.
3. The government has introduced computer classes in schools. Companies are working with academic institutions so that graduating students will have skills tailored to the job market.
4. The Nano is an icon of Indian ingenuity and entrepreneurialism. Selling for just 100,000 rupees ($2,100), it seeks to reach a new class of customers through frugal engineering.
5. Many had refused the compensation the state government offered when it hurriedly expropriated their land to make room for the Tata Motors plant.

FICHE 4

Méthode
La note de synthèse

La note de synthèse est une note rédigée, structurée montrant les capacités du rédacteur à organiser ses idées de manière logique.

1 Comment rédiger une note de synthèse

A. Les généralités

• Il ne s'agit pas de résumer chacun des documents, il s'agit d'une argumentation basée sur une problématique.
• Il ne s'agit pas non plus d'un commentaire ni d'une explication de textes.
• La note de synthèse comporte trois parties : introduction, développement et conclusion.
• Il s'agit de dégager les idées principales en lien avec la question posée et les regrouper de manière logique.

B. Les différentes étapes d'une note de synthèse

1. Première étape

Il faut bien lire et analyser le sujet, car il faut comprendre le problème posé.

2. Deuxième étape

Il s'agit de la lecture approfondie des textes et/ou des images, avec prise de notes, afin de faire une sélection des idées se rapportant directement au sujet. Lors de cette étape, il vous faut relire régulièrement le sujet afin de bien le garder à l'esprit.
Il faut donc repérer les idées qui ont un rapport entre elles.

• **Exemple**

► **Document : *Outsourcing Works, So India Is Exporting Jobs***

One of the constants of the global economy has been companies moving their tasks – and jobs – to India.
Most of Infosys's 75,000 employees are Indians, in India. They ***account for most of the company's $3.1 billion in sales*** in the year that ended March 31, from work for clients like **Bank of America and Goldman Sachs**.
India continues to be the No. 1 location for outsourcing.

► **Document : *India's Outsourcing Industry Is Facing a Labor Shortage***

India's $23.4 billion outsourcing industry accounts for most of the country's software and services industry, ***which makes up nearly 5 percent of gross domestic product***. The industry employs 1.2 million workers, has sparked a consumer revolution in India, and is accelerating at more than 30 percent a year.

• Les idées sont d'abord repérées :
- companies outsource to India
- ***Indian companies make money thanks to outsourcing***
- **they have American clients**
- *India is the first country to benefit from outsourcing*
- ***the IT industry participates in the Indian GDP***
- the companies employ a lot of workers, Indian workers

• Elles sont ensuite organisées en un paragraphe dans la note de synthèse :
As far as IT is concerned, India is *the first location for outsourcing* and a lot of companies have benefited from globalisation. Their ambition is to get work from the West done in India. IT firms work for numerous important **American clients**, for example, and employ a great number of employees. ***Their sales account for an important part of India's GDP.***

3. Troisième étape

Elle concerne la construction du plan détaillé avec éventuellement le titre des parties. Cohérent et bien construit, le plan est essentiel dans la note de synthèse. Il arrive souvent que la question posée vous oriente vers un plan.

• **Exemple**
« Rédigez une note de synthèse en anglais (350 mots) en synthétisant les éléments du dossier pour mettre en évidence les conséquences variées de la mondialisation en Inde ».
Ce sujet vous oriente vers un plan dans lequel vous devrez faire état des conséquences de la mondialisation en Inde. Vous pouvez donc essayer de voir quels sont les aspects positifs (*cf.* paragraphe précédent) et les aspects négatifs de la mondialisation ou les freins à celle-ci.

4. Quatrième étape

Il s'agit de la relecture des textes et de l'ajout des idées manquantes dans le plan.

5. Cinquième étape

Il faut rédiger les différentes parties :
– l'introduction : elle situe l'intérêt du sujet par rapport à l'actualité ou par rapport à l'histoire, elle constitue l'accroche. Elle définit le cadre exact de la question posée et annonce la problématique et le plan ;
– le développement : il comporte 2 ou 3 parties. Un plan comportant deux parties est peut-être plus facile pour équilibrer les parties ;
– la conclusion : elle apporte une réponse à la problématique posée.

6. Sixième étape

La relecture est importante, elle est indispensable pour éviter les erreurs de base.

C. La rédaction de la note de synthèse

Elle doit privilégier la précision, doit comporter des mots de liaison et les transitions entre paragraphes.
Il vaut mieux ne pas recopier de passages des textes (sauf s'ils sont indispensables à l'argumentation).

Exercice 4.1

À partir des documents de la Fiche 3 : rédigez une note de synthèse en anglais (350 mots) en synthétisant les éléments du dossier pour mettre en évidence les conséquences variées de la mondialisation en Inde.

FICHE 5

La constitution d'espaces économiques régionaux : l'Europe

1 Ground work

Trade blocs

A **trade bloc** is a type of intergovernmental agreement, often part of a regional intergovernmental organization, where regional barriers to trade (tariff (1) and non-tariff barriers) are reduced or eliminated among the participating states.

By 1997, more than 50% of all world commerce was conducted under the auspices of regional trade blocs. Members of successful trade blocs usually share four common traits: similar levels of per capita GNP (2), geographic proximity, similar or compatible trading regimes, and political commitment (3) to regional organization.

Advocates (4) of worldwide free trade are generally opposed to trading blocs, which, they argue, encourage regional as opposed to global free trade. Scholars and economists continue to debate whether regional trade blocs are leading to a more fragmented world economy or encouraging the extension of the existing global multilateral trading system. Trade blocs can be stand-alone (5) agreements between several states (such as the **North American Free Trade Agreement** (NAFTA) or part of a regional organization (such as the **European Union**). Depending on the level of economic integration, trade blocs can fall into different categories, such as: preferential trading areas, free trade areas, customs unions (6), common markets and economic and monetary unions.

► **Different types of trade blocs**

Regional trading blocs are often known as Regional Integration Agreements (RIAs).

In a Free Trade Area (FTA), countries are free to set their own external trade policy, whereas in a Customs Union (CU), the RIA as a whole sets a common external policy. A CU typically requires greater political commitment.

The European Union has played a large role in the surge of activity, with the implementation of the Single Market Program in 1992; enlargement of its membership, and numerous agreements with other countries. These agreements account for (7) two-thirds of the agreements notified to GATT (8)/WTO (9) since 1990, include the European Economic Area, the Europe Agreements with countries of Eastern Europe, the EU-Turkey Customs Union, and the development of a Mediterranean policy.

The European Free Trade Association (EFTA): today, only Iceland, Norway, Switzerland, and Liechtenstein remain members of EFTA (of which only Norway and Switzerland are the only remaining founding members). The Stockholm Convention provides for the liberalisation of trade among the member states.

Three of the EFTA countries are part of the European Union Internal Market through the Agreement on a European Economic Area (EEA), which took effect in 1994; the fourth, Switzerland, opted to conclude bilateral agreements with the EU. In addition, the EFTA states have jointly concluded free trade agreements with a number of other countries.

In Latin America, MERCOSUR (Mercado Comùn del Sur), an RTA between Argentina, Brazil, Paraguay and Uruguay was formed in 1991 and the Group of Three in 1995, the Andean Pact and Central America Common Market (CACM). Its purpose is to promote free trade and the fluid movement of goods, people, and currency. Bolivia, Chile, Colombia, Ecuador and Peru currently have associate member status. Venezuela signed a membership agreement on 17 June 2006.

In Sub-Saharan Africa, the blocs in West Africa were reformed. The South African Development Community (SADC) supplemented by the Cross-border Initiative. The 9 founding states are: Angola, Botswana, Lesotho, Malawi, Mozambique, Swaziland, Tanzania, Zambia and Zimbabwe. Now it includes 15 members.

The Middle-East witnessed the development of the Gulf Cooperation Council (GCC) in 1997. Arab League members agreed to cut trade barriers (10) over a 10-year period.

In Asia, the Association of Southeast Asian Nations (ASEAN) developed 25 years of political cooperation into a FTA in 1991, with the formation of the ASEAN Free Trade Area. It includes Thailand, Indonesia, Singapore, the Philippines, Cambodia, Malaysia, Vietnam, etc. The South Asian free Trade area is, in terms of population, the world's largest regional agreement.

In 1994, the Canada-US FTA was extended to Mexico through NAFTA. For the first time a developing country joined industrial countries as an equal partner in a trade bloc designed to bolster (11) economic development in all three economies.

Links between high-income and developing economies have also been forged in the Asia Pacific Economic Cooperation (APEC) established in 1989. For example they have taken the lead in formulating (12) and articulating the position of the African Caribbean and Pacific countries group and negotiating the Lomé convention. The clearest example of regional solidarity with the objective of getting noticed is the Caribbean Community and Common Market (CARICOM), not focused on achieving regional integration as its objective is rather common action.

Strong ties are established between high-income countries (such as EU or the EE Area), some between middle-income such as MERCOSUR or the ASEAN FTA, some low-income (the West African economic and monetary union (13)) contains a mixture of incomes with a high-income partner (NAFTA or the EU).

1. *tariff barrier* : barrière douanière ou tarifaire – *non-tariff barrier* : barrière non tarifaire
2. *per capita GNP* : produit national brut (PNB) par habitant
3. *commitment* : engagement
4. *advocates* : défenseurs, partisans
5. *stand-alone* : autonome
6. *customs union* : union douanière
7. *to account for* : représenter, expliquer
8. *GATT* : General Agreement on Tariffs and trade
9. *WTO* : World Trade Organisation: Organisation mondiale du commerce (OMC)
10. *trade barrier* : barrière douanière
11. *to bolster = boost* : renforcer, relancer
12. *formulate* : formuler, élaborer
13. *the West African economic and monetary union* : l'Union économique et monétaire ouest-africaine.

2 Zooming on

Winners and losers

Europe is a big winner from globalisation. If onlypoliticians would say so.

[…] Half a century on, a growing body of research makes the case that, contrary to widespread belief, globalisation has made life better for most European citizens. What is more, Europe is unusually good at it. Yet political leaders seem wary of delivering the good news. With few exceptions, the political rhetoric when it comes to globalisation ranges from grim resolve (this challenge can be managed) to plain grim (we must tame this menace). Defending globalisation is left to a cottage industry of think-tanks, academics and business lobbies (although some of the most thoughtful studies are quietly financed by pro-market governments, from Finland to the Netherlands, or by the European Union).

What is going on? Politics, mostly. Today's Europeans fear that globalisation may not be good for most people. Or, to be more precise, even if they notice the diffuse benefits (cheap jeans and hightech gadgets), they fret about the visible losers, starting with workers whose jobs are shipped overseas. Worse, with globalisation disrupting business models at an ever finer level of detail many citizens feel they cannot be sure if they will be next.

A new book by a pair of academics from America's Johns Hopkins University finds lots of facts to cheer Europeans up. European consumers (ie, all Europeans when they are shopping) are big winners from globalisation, which has delivered cheap imports, held down inflation and kept interest rates low. Despite the fuss about China and India, the EU's share of world exports rose slightly between 2000 and 2006. What is more, two-thirds of Chinese exports involve foreign brands, a good chunk of which are European. Nor does a "made in China" tag mean big revenues for Chinese firms. In a recent speech defending globalisation, the EU trade commissioner, Peter Mandelson, cited a University of California study into who gains when an iPod is sold in America for $299. Only $4 stays in China with the firms that assemble the devices, Mr Mandelson explained. $160 goes to American companies that design, transport and retail iPods. A similar pattern holds for many European products. Europeans worry a lot about wage competition.

The researchers note that globalisation is not just about wages, but more broadly about finding efficiencies anywhere along complex supply chains. After all, most non-EU employees of European firms live in America, not China (EU and Swiss firms employ some 3.5m workers in America). Yes, European jobs have been lost by offshoring, but unevenly. In France only 3.4% of jobs lost in 2005 could be blamed on offshoring, though there has been a wave of factory closures more recently. Portugal has suffered more: a quarter of its job losses between 2003 and 2006 involved jobs heading overseas, mostly to new EU members.

Stick to the data, and globalisation Angst in Europe can look like the tail wagging the dog. Italian producers have demanded anti-dumping duties of tens of millions of euros on Chinese air compressors, to preserve just 500 jobs. Yet in a political world, data get you only so far. A politician seen as heartless towards 500 workers risks punishment by millions of watching voters. EU economies may have created 18m more jobs than they shed in the past decade. But the jobs are different: like America, Europe has shed manufacturing and farming jobs, and created new ones in services. Many Europeans suspect these of being precarious and lowpaid. […]

The Economist, February 28th, 2008, by Charlemagne

Useful language

to abide by : respecter
agenda : programme
applicant countries : pays candidats
attitude : mentalité
to be plagued with : souffrir de
to boost growth : stimuler la croissance
border : frontière
Charter of Human Rights : Charte des droits fondamentaux
to come into force : entrer en vigueur
commitment : engagement
competitiveness : compétitivité
to comply with rules : se plier aux règles
cultural mix : mélange culturel
to devise : élaborer
to draft : ébaucher
to ease/to lift/to reinforce controls : assouplir/lever/renforcer les contrôles
enlargement : élargissement
entitlement : droits sociaux
European Central Bank : Banque Centrale Européenne
European MP : député européen
European Parliament : Parlement européen
European Union (EU) : Union européenne (EU)
eurosceptics : eurosceptiques
expatriate : expatrié
fellow citizen : concitoyen
fiscal/social policy : politique fiscale/sociale
foreign policy : politique étrangère
GDP(Gross Domestic Product) : PIB (Produit Intérieur Brut)
to grant (asylum) : accorder le droit d'asile
growth rate : taux de croissance
home country : pays d'origine
host country : pays d'accueil
to implement a policy : mettre en œuvre une politique
import levy : prélèvement à l'importation
imports/exports : importations/exportations
incentive : mesure d'incitation
income tax : impôts sur le revenu
to join/to enter : adhérer à/entrer
to leave one's country : s'expatrier
to liberalise : libéraliser
membership : appartenance
migration policy : politique d'immigration
negotiations/talks : négociation
patent : brevet
to push for unification : promouvoir l'unification
retaliatory measure : mesure de rétorsion
scheme : plan, projet
scholarship : bourse d'études
single currency : devise unique
single market : marché unique
social security : déductions/prélèvements sociaux

social welfare system : system système de protection sociale
standard of living :niveau de vie
state aid :subvention de l'état
to subsidise : subventionner
subsidy : subvention
summit : sommet, réunion
to take in immigrants : accueillir des immigrants
taxation : fiscalité
think tank : cellule de réflexion
trade : échanges commerciaux
treaty : traité
way of life/lifestyle : mode de vie
welfare state : État providence

3 Comprehension of document

Exercice 5.1

Donnez le mot correspondant à la définition.

1. to give money
2. money given to a student
3. a country that would like to join
4. the euro is one
5. people who don't really believe in Europe's strength
6. some were signed in Rome, Maastricht, Nice, Lisbon
7. to accept foreign people
8. a group of people who try to find ideas
9. to give foreign people who face problems in their country the right to stay
10. the line between two countries

Exercice 5.2

Traduisez en anglais.

1. Les pays candidats à l'adhésion de l'Union européenne doivent respecter les Droits de l'Homme.
2. Le sommet de Lisbonne a eu lieu en 2007.
3. Des bourses d'étude sont accordées aux étudiants pour faciliter leur mobilité.
4. La politique étrangère commune est élaborée par tous les pays membres.
5. Les Européens craignent la mondialisation et s'inquiètent pour leurs emplois.

FICHE 6

Méthode
Le résumé

Le résumé est la réduction d'un document où les idées, les arguments, etc., sont exprimés en un minimum de mots : le texte est recomposé. En outre, le résumé doit aller à l'essentiel.

1 Les grands principes du résumé

Le résumé réduit le texte de départ selon les principes suivants.

- **La longueur**

En général, on réduit le texte à peu près au tiers de sa longueur de départ. Il convient bien sûr, si l'énoncé l'indique, de respecter le nombre de mots demandés (une marge de plus ou mois 10 % est généralement tolérée, voire même indiquée).

- **La source**

Ne citez pas le nom de l'auteur du texte ni la source de celui-ci.

- **L'ordre**

Suivez l'ordre chronologique du texte : ne faites ni introduction ni conclusion.

- **Le point de vue**

Soyez objectif : ne donnez pas votre opinion, respectez le point de vue de l'auteur. Limitez les exemples : seuls ceux indispensables à la compréhension peuvent être repris.

2 La méthode pas à pas

A. Lecture du texte

Vous devez lire plusieurs fois le texte afin d'en comprendre le sens général ainsi que les idées essentielles.

B. Le repérage

Il faut commencer par souligner les idées essentielles et les mots clés, puis repérer les mots de liaison, **les mots indiquant une chronologie** ; ils sont importants car ils indiquent la relation entre les idées.

- **Exemple**

Half a century on, a growing body of research makes the case that, contrary to widespread belief, globalisation has made life better for most European citizens. What is more, Europe is unusually good at it. Yet political leaders seem wary of delivering the good news. With few exceptions, the political rhetoric when it comes to globalisation ranges from grim resolve (this challenge can be managed) to plain grim (we must tame this menace). Defending globalisation is left to a cottage industry of think-tanks, academics and business lobbies (although some of the most thoughtful studies are quietly financed by pro-market governments, from Finland to the Netherlands, or by the European Union).

Remarque. *Dans ce premier paragraphe, comme c'est habituellement le cas, l'auteur présente le thème et donc beaucoup de mots et d'idées sont soulignés.*

Exercice 6.1

1. Soulignez les idées principales du paragraphe suivant.

2. Repérez les mots indiquant une chronologie et indiquez également les mots de liaison. Faites la rédaction du résumé.

A new book by a pair of academics from America's Johns Hopkins University finds lots of facts to cheer Europeans up. European consumers (ie, all Europeans when they are shopping) are big winners from globalisation, which has delivered cheap imports, held down inflation and kept interest rates low. Despite the fuss about China and India, the EU's share of world exports rose slightly between 2000 and 2006. What is more, two-thirds of Chinese exports involve foreign brands, a good chunk of which are European. Nor does a "made in China" tag mean big revenues for Chinese firms. In a recent speech defending globalisation, the EU trade commissioner, Peter Mandelson, cited a University of California study into who gains when an iPod is sold in America for $299. Only $4 stays in China with the firms that assemble the devices, Mr Mandelson explained. $160 goes to American companies that design, transport and retail iPods. A similar pattern holds for many European products.

C. La rédaction

Vous devez reformuler les idées du texte dans vos propres termes. Pour ce faire, utilisez une langue claire, concise et variée. Utilisez des mots de liaison et des phrases complexes.

Pensez à vérifier la qualité de l'expression et à indiquer le nombre de mots utilisés en fin de travail.

Exercice 6.2

Rédigez le résumé en anglais de l'article *Winners and losers* de la Fiche 5.

FICHE 7

Les technologies de l'information et de la communication

1 Ground work

Information and Communication Technology

Information and Communication Technology or **ICTs** allow users to participate in a rapidly changing world in which work and other activities are increasingly transformed by access to varied and developing technologies. ICT tools can be used to find, explore, analyze, exchange and present information responsibly and without discrimination. Technology is at the heart of the digital networked economy – one that is defined by low cost connectivity and the convergence of IT & Communications. ICT can be employed to give users quick access to ideas and experiences from a wide range of people, communities and cultures. This illustrates the great potential of the **information society**.

▸ Social impacts

ICTs have impacted societies on many levels. They have extended the reach of public administration, leading to a centralization of regional management into urban centres.

Despite the international spread (1) of ICTs, the economic impacts have been geographically uneven (2). They have exacerbated pre-existing disparities between developed countries, which can afford to produce and consume the latest technologies, and developing countries, which cannot. This gap is known as the digital divide (3) within all its aspects: technological, territorial, social, cultural, and linguistic.

The diffusion of ICTs within societies is varied, with some institutions and sections of society having greater access to ICTs than others. These divisions are reflected in the content of ICTs. For example the English language, which is understood by only 10% of the world's population, accounts for approximately 80% of internet content.

Despite these imbalances (4) in power relations, many social justice movements believe ICTs can be used to promote equality and empower (5) marginalized and disadvantaged groups. These groups advocate ICTs as a means of providing accessible and affordable information and as a platform for voices that might otherwise go unheard.

As a major donor of economic aid, the EU has an inclusive approach, and stresses ICTs' key role in fostering economic development assistance and co-operation programmes, as illustrated by the EU Growth Initiative.

A significant achievement of the World Summit on the Information Society (WSIS) (6) could be an international commitment to notably increasing the effort the North is dedicating to research on ICTs to help bridge (7) the "digital divide" with the South. One key issue is internet access. A second challenge is the need for ICTs tailored (8) to the needs and conditions of the poor in the developing world.

Achieving this, however, will not only mean providing countries in the South with the technical means of participating in the international **knowledge revolution**. Most personal computers, for example, are built for individuals who are both literate and numerate (9). Such preconditions can be taken for granted in most developed nations, but they are far from the case in the rest of the world.

So, although ICTs have come to play an essential role in a wide range of development strategies, the link between the potential and the reality remains fragile.

▸ Economic development

ICTs facilitate the ease of communication, which has many profound effects. In the business world, deals can be made through **emails**, using new technologies such as **voice activated programmes, desktop video conferencing**, and **mobile phone** technology has made it possible for people to check and send messages on the go (10), allowing us to be connected 24-7. The considerable increase in the proportion of business connected by broadband shows that companies are embracing the opportunities that ICT can bring. It is particularly encouraging to see that small businesses are beginning to narrow the digital divide that appeared to have opened up in recent years.

Although this has greatly facilitated the business world in general, many negative implications have to be considered as well. Simple messages which used to be delivered face-to-face are now being sent through the cold impersonal means of email. This has effectively reduced socialisation within the office, thus contributing to the weakening of bonds (11) within the workplace.

Moreover, ICT is a tool of ever increasing importance in today's fast moving business world. Good, effective communication allows organizations to gain commercial advantage by sharing knowledge and expertise in a timely (12), efficient way. It brings people together to communicate and collaborate for mutual benefit. Technology is at the heart of the digital networked economy – one that is defined by low cost connectivity and the convergence of IT & Communications.

ICTs have led to new forms of employment in innovation and production of ICTs and a demand for highly-skilled specialists. However, ICTs have also enabled professionals in certain industries to be replaced by unskilled workers, or even made entirely redundant (13). Proponents (14) of ICTs portray this as a 're-skilling' (15) of the workforce, while to detractors it is a 'de-skilling' (16) process.

ICTs have been identified by many international development institutions as a crucial element in developing the worlds' poorest countries, by integrating them into the global economy and by making global markets more accessible. **The World Bank** has collaborated with **the International Finance Corporation** to promote access to ICTs, an initiative which it describes as one of its most successful. In 2006, the **United Nations** launched an initiative called the **Global Alliance for Information and Communication Technologies and Development.** There are calls to substitute the concept of digital divide with the more positive term "digital solidarity". This challenge will constitute one of the priorities for international action and it is already at the heart of the EU's concerns.

Just as is the case with the aerospace industry, the computer industry has long been driven by one concern – performance. But the better the performance, the more energy it needs.

So data (17) centres – the heart of computer networks worldwide – have a vast and ever-increasing appetite for power: ICTs emit 2% of total CO_2 emissions, though there are signs that the ICT industry is changing. UN data suggests that the manufacture of one computer uses 75 times its weight in raw materials and water. Let alone the energy used over the lifetime of a computer. The need for change is clear.

1. *spread* : diffusion, propagation
2. *uneven* : irrégulier, inégal

3. *the digital divide* : la fracture numérique
4. *imbalance* : déséquilibre (substantif)
5. *to empower* : autoriser, habiliter
6. *WSIS* : le sommet mondial sur la société de l'information
7. *to bridge* : combler
8. *tailored* : adapté à, conçu pour
9. *literate and numerate* : sachant lire et compter
10. *on the go* : dans la foulée
11. *bonds* : liens, rapports
12. *timely* : opportun
13. *to be made redundant* : être licencié, mis au chômage
14. *proponents* : partisans
15. *re-skilling* : requalifier
16. *de-skilling* : déqualifier
17. *data* : données (singulier : datum)

2 Zooming on

OECD proposes roadmap for the *future* of the Internet economy

18/06/2008 – The OECD is to work with developed and developing countries and international organisations to improve *policies* for *the Internet* economy and increase international co-operation on issues such as cybercrime and *security*.

OECD member *countries*, the European Community and ministers from Chile, Egypt, Estonia, India, Indonesia, Israel, Latvia, Senegal and Slovenia affirmed in a declaration their commitment to working together to stimulate innovation, competition and investment in information and communications technology. Their ultimate goal is to build *confidence* in and secure the future of the Internet economy.

The Seoul Declaration came at the close of the OECD Ministerial Meeting on the Future of the Internet Economy, held in Seoul, Korea, on 17-18 June 2008. Participants agreed on the need for governments to work closely with business, civil society and technical experts on policies that promote competition, empower and protect consumers, and expand Internet access and use *worldwide*.

"Given that this infrastructure has become *critical* to our economies and societies, we *should* all engage in developing better, more broad-based, governance arrangements and policies," said *OECD Secretary-General Angel Gurría* in the closing session […]

He called for a new approach to drawing up these policies. "A more decentralised, networked approach to policy formulation for the Internet economy that includes the active participation of stakeholders."

It had been 10 years since the landmark Ottawa OECD Ministerial Meeting on E-Commerce, he said, *but* "we cannot talk about the importance of the Internet every ten years which is an eternity in Internet time." He pledged to review progress on the Declaration within three years.

The Declaration sets out a roadmap to upgrade the communication policies that have helped the Internet become the economic driver that it is today and ensure that they support its future development. Governments and business should work together to leverage technology more effectively and creatively to help tackle global long-term challenges such as climate change, the Declaration states.

During the closing session of the Ministerial, the OECD committed to improving statistical indicators to measure access and use of the Internet and its networks in order to provide more reliable data and analysis, notably of the impact of the Internet on economic performance and social well-being.

The OECD agreed to work closely with stakeholders to increase *confidence* in the Internet, to protect users online more effectively and enhance the fight against cyberthreats through improved cross-border co-operation. The organisation would also assess how OECD instruments related to competition, consumer protection, privacy and security are being applied by governments and business.

oecd.org

Useful language

access : avoir accès à/accès
available on line : disponible sur Interner
to browse, to surf : naviguer sur Internet
a browser : un navigateur
to chat :discuter
a chat room : un forum de discussion
computer-friendly : convivial
computer scientist : informaticien
to click : cliquer
cookies : programmes espions
cybercrime : cyber-criminalité
cybercriminal : pirate informatique
cybermarket : cybermarché
data (invariable) : données
database : base de données
delete : effacer
digital camera : appareil photo numérique
dotcom company : entreprise commerciale sur Internet
to download : télécharger
e-business, e-commerce : commerce électronique
encrypted : codé
hacker : pirate informatique
hardware : matériel
homepage : page d'accueil d'un site
hotline : assistance téléphonique
ICT : Information and Communication Technologies
internet user : internaute, cybernaute
keyboard : clavier
laptop computer : ordinateur portable
link : lien
to load : charger
log-in : identifiant
mobile phone, cell phone : téléphone portable
a monitor : un écran
to monitor : contrôler
mouse : souris
network : réseau
online shopping : achats sur Internet
password : mot de passe
printer : imprimante
privacy : vie privée

provider : fournisseur d'accès
to save, to store : sauvegarder
screen : flat panel screen
écran : écran plat
search engine : moteur de recherche
to share files : partager des fichiers
shareware : logiciel de partage de fichiers
software : logiciel
spam, electronic junk mail : multipostage électronique abusif
spreadsheet : tableur
teleworking : télétravail
text message : SMS, texto
to upgrade, to update : actualiser, améliorer
user-friendly : convivial
voicemail : messagerie vocale
webcam : camera web
web designer : créateur de site Internet
wired : branché
wireless : sans fil
word processing : traitement de texte
World Wide Web : toile mondiale, web

3 Comprehension of document

Exercice 7.1

Donnez les mots correspondant aux définitions.

1. A small computer that you can carry everywhere.
2. A written message sent with a cell phone.
3. A group of computers that are connected.
4. Someone who creates websites.
5. To improve your system.
6. Google is probably the most famous.
7. A piece of software you need to calculate.
8. A device without wires.
9. A software you use to type your homework with.
10. All the information in your computer.

Exercice 7.2

Traduisez en français.

1. Cyber-criminals steal data.
2. Wireless phones are more user-friendly.
3. You need a password to download this software.
4. I must upgrade my hardware and buy a new printer.
5. There was a crash on the dotcom companies in the 80's.

FICHE 8

Méthode
La traduction

La traduction en français est un exercice qui exige à la fois une bonne connaissance de la langue anglaise et une bonne maîtrise de la langue française. Elle demande à la fois rigueur, concentration et connaissance de techniques précises.

1 Comment traduire un texte ?

A. Première étape

Il vous faut lire plusieurs fois le texte attentivement et l'analyser pour bien en saisir le thème et l'argumentation (l'idée principale et les idées secondaires). Certains indices peuvent apporter des précisions intéressantes :
- la source, l'auteur, la date de publication ;
- le sens global ;
- le point de vue ;
- l'organisation du texte (logique, chronologique…).

B. La compréhension du texte (d'une compréhension globale à une compréhension détaillée)

1. Les mots inconnus

Ne cherchez pas à faire une liste des mots inconnus. Tentez plutôt de repérer :
- les mots transparents ;

• **Exemple**
Future → le futur, *security* → la sécurité

- les mots que vous connaissez ;

• **Exemple**
Countries → les pays

- les mots composés *(compound words)* ;

• **Exemple**
Developed countries → les pays développés
Developing countries → les pays en voie de développement
Climate change → le changement climatique

Exercice 8.1

1. Donnez la traduction des mots.

2. Essayez ensuite de déduire le sens de ceux que vous ne connaissez pas.

1. a roadmap (title)
2. member countries
3. empower
4. governance arrangements
5. closing session

– les faux amis.

• **Exemple**
Policies → les politiques
Confidence → la confiance
Critical → vital/fondamental (dans ce contexte)

Exercice 8.2

Déduisez le sens des mots.
1. issues
2. goal
3. stakeholders
4. to leverage
5. enhance

Repérez également :
– les mots de liaison ;

• **Exemple**
But → mais (il y a donc une opposition entre les deux parties de la phrase)

– les verbes et leurs temps et/ou aspects ;

• **Exemple**
*That **have helped*** → qui **ont aidé/contribué** (present perfect = action commencée dans le passé qui continue dans le présent)

– les auxiliaires modaux ;

• **Exemple**
*We **should** all engage...* → nous **devrions** tous nous attacher à... (*should* = idée de conseil)

– les prépositions, etc.

• **Exemple**
*Critical **to**...* → vital **pour**...

2. Les phrases

Découpez les phrases en unités de sens. Si le texte comporte des phrases complexes, tâchez de retrouver la phrase minimale.

• **Exemple**
The Declaration sets out a roadmap *to upgrade* the communication policies// *that have helped the Internet become the economic driver/that it is today*// ***and ensure that*** they ***support its future development.***
Traduction :
La Déclaration établit une feuille de route *pour moderniser* les politiques de communication// *qui ont contribué à faire de l'Internet le moteur économique qu'il est devenu aujourd'hui*// ***et faire en sorte que*** celles-ci ***facilitent son développement futur***

Remarque : *Les découpages correspondent aux différentes unités de sens.*

Exercice 8.3

1. Coupez la phrase de façon à mettre en valeur les groupes de mots.

2. Traduisez-la en français.

The OECD is to work with developed and developing countries and international organisations to improve policies for the Internet economy and increase international co-operation on issues such as cyber-crime and security.

3. Les titres

Afin de rendre les titres plus concis et plus lapidaires, les journaux emploient une syntaxe et un vocabulaire particuliers :

• Les mots moins importants sont supprimés.

• **Exemple**

4 killed in Plane Crash → 4 people were killed in a plane crash

L'article *a* et l'auxiliaire *were* sont effacés, ainsi que *people* qui contient peu d'information.

• Les **références au temps** se réduisent à trois formes :

– le **présent simple** correspond au présent et au passé ;

• **Exemple**

Oil Breaks New Records

– le **participe passé** correspond au présent ou au passé ;

• **Exemple**

Journalists held hostage (présent)

Further increases expected (passé)

– **to + infinitif** correspond au futur.

• **Exemple**

Eu to sign agreement

• La ponctuation est particulière :

– le point d'interrogation s'utilise afin d'exprimer le doute ;

• **Exemple**

Petrol to reach £5 a gallon? → Petrol may reach £5 a gallon

– *and* est remplacé par une **virgule**.

• **Exemple**

Aer Lingus, Ryanair back the proposition → Aer Lingus and Ryanair are supporting the proposition

• Le **premier mot** du titre est **toujours en majuscules**, et tous les autres mots aussi dans les journaux américains. Exception faite des prépositions constitués d'une syllabe, des conjonctions et des articles.

• **Exemple**

A WATERSHED in the WORKPLACE

• Des mots courts qui font gagner de la place remplacent les mots plus longs.

• **Exemple**

John Childs denied he is intending to merge with Capos → John Childs: No Merger

Exercice 8.4

Faites des phrases complètes à partir de ces titres.

1. U.S.: Higher Tariffs on Oil, Textiles?
2. Output up
3. Exports £60 million
4. Unemployment: No Change
5. John Peters: No Merger
6. Inflation down
7. Mass Production of Petrol-Free Cars to Start in Japan

Exercice 8.5

Transformez les phrases suivantes en titres.

1. Merger negotiations between Khian Sea and Oileak have floundered.
2. Radon may be responsible for lung cancer.
3. Mr Thomas MacEnroe said thousands of families would suffer if the car plant closed.
4. President Obama has said he would support trade negotiations at the start of the summit.
5. Nestle may sell its subsidiary.
6. Ron Anders and Richard Grayson are backing Paul Graham.
7. An Egyptian has been sentenced in a terrorism case.

C. La traduction

1. Conseils généraux

- Ne vous contentez pas d'un premier jet trop approximatif.
- N'omettez aucun mot. Tenez donc compte de tous les mots sans pour autant tomber dans le calque maladroit.
- Ne donnez pas deux traductions possibles. C'est votre version, c'est à vous de faire le choix, de trouver le mot juste.
- Traduisez le titre (et les éventuels sous-titres) après avoir traduit tout le texte, afin d'éviter les contresens et de trouver le ton juste.
- Vérifiez que votre traduction est sensée et cohérente et que vous n'avez pas dévié de l'idée directrice de l'article.

2. Que faut-il traduire ? Ou ne pas traduire ?

- Ne pas traduire noms et prénoms.

• Exemple
Angel Gurría → Angel Gurria

Exceptions : les noms de souverains.
Exemple : *Queen Elizabeth* → la reine Elisabeth

- Ne pas traduire les noms de sociétés ou les titres de presse.

• Exemple
National Foods, Cadbury, The Observer, The Independent

- Traduire les titres.

• Exemple
OECD ***Secretary-General*** → le **secrétaire général** de l'OCDE

- Traduire les noms géographiques.

- **Exemple**
Latvia, Senegal → la Lettonie, le Sénégal

- Convertir les mesures.

- **Exemple**
Miles → kilomètres

Rappel : *1 mile = 1,6 km*

- Traduire les devises mais ne pas les convertir.

- **Exemple**
Twelve ***pounds*** → douze **livres sterling** (ne pas convertir en euros)

3. Les techniques de traduction

a. La traduction littérale, le calque

Ce type de traduction est à employer à chaque fois que cela est possible à condition de rester vigilant. Il est important d'apprendre à éviter le calque et à chercher les diverses possibilités de se détacher du texte anglais.

- **Exemple**
The Declaration sets out a roadmap... → La Déclaration établit une feuille de route...

b. L'emprunt

- **Exemple**
The Internet → Internet

c. La transposition

On effectue un changement de catégorie grammaticale.

- **Exemple**
He called for a new approach ***to drawing up*** *these policies* → Il a appelé à une nouvelle approche **dans la formulation** de ces politiques (verbe devenant un nom).
To leverage technology more ***effectively*** *and* creatively → pour tirer un parti plus **efficace** et plus **créatif** de la technologie (adverbes devenant des adjectifs).

d. La modulation

- On effectue une inversion du point de vue.

- **Exemple**
Lost Property Office → Bureau des objets trouvés
Work to rule → grève du zèle
Moonlighting → le travail au noir
The grass root → la base (dans le contexte d'un syndicat)

- On effectue une double inversion.

- **Exemple**
It does 15 miles to the gallon → Elle consomme 20 litres au cent

- On donne le contraire de la négation.

- **Exemple**
No vacancies → Complet

e. L'équivalence

Surtout pour la traduction de proverbes, d'expressions idiomatiques…

- **Exemple**
It's raining cats and dogs → Il tombe des cordes
No U turning → Interdit de faire demi-tour

f. L'étoffement

Il est souvent obligatoire.

- **Exemple**
worldwide → à l'échelle mondiale

4. La relecture

- Vérifiez l'orthographe.
- Vérifiez la ponctuation.
- Contrôlez si vous avez bien traduit le titre car vous avez peut-être fait un contresens au départ et vous le découvrirez une fois parvenu à la fin de votre version du texte.
- Relisez votre texte pour évaluer la qualité du français et développer votre sens critique. Une relecture à voix basse, plutôt qu'une relecture des yeux vous permettra d'évaluer l'agencement de votre message et sa cohérence dans le temps imparti.

Exercice 8.6

Traduisez le texte du document *OECD proposes roadmap for the future of the Internet economy* de la Fiche 7 (Les technologies de l'information et de la communication).

FICHE 9

La concurrence et le droit

1 Ground work

Competition Law

Competition law means laws that promote or maintain market competition (1) by regulating anti-competitive conduct (2).

The business practices of market traders, guilds (3) and governments have always been subject to scrutiny, and sometimes severe sanctions. Since the twentieth century, competition law has become global. The two largest and most influential systems of competition regulation (4) are **United States antitrust law** and **European Union competition law**. National and regional competition authorities across the world have formed international support and enforcement (5) networks.

▸ 1. European Union competition law is one of the areas of authority of the European Union.

Competition law regulates the exercise of market power by large companies, governments or other economic entities. In the EU, it is an important part of ensuring the completion (6) of the internal market, meaning the free flow of working people, goods, services and capital in a borderless Europe. Four main policy areas include:

- Cartels, or control of collusion (7) and other anti-competitive practices which has an effect on the EU (or, since 1994, the European Economic Area).
- Monopolies or preventing the abuse (8) of firms' dominant market positions.

This also gives rise to the Commission's authority on :

- Mergers, control of proposed mergers, acquisitions and joint ventures (9) involving companies which have a certain, defined amount of turnover in the EU/EEA.
- State aid (10), control of direct and indirect aid given by Member States of the European Union to companies.

This last point is a unique characteristic of the EU competition law regime. As the EU is made up of independent member states, both competition policy and the creation of the European single market could be rendered ineffective were member states free to support national companies as they saw fit. Primary competence for applying EU competition law rests with the **European Commission** and its **Directorate General for Competition**.

▸ 2. Competition law is known in the United States as antitrust law

Competition law has already been substantially internationalised along the lines of the US model by nation states themselves. However, the involvement of international organisations has been growing increasingly active at all international conferences, such as the United Nations Conference on Trade and Development (UNCTAD) and the Organisation for Economic Co-operation and Development (OECD), which is prone to making neo-liberal recommendations about the total application of competition law for public and private industries.

The protection of international competition is governed by international competition agreements. In 1945, during the negotiations preceding the adoption of the General Agreement on Tariffs and Trade (GATT) in 1947, limited international competition obligations were proposed within the Charter for an International Trade Organisation. These obligations were not included in GATT, but in 1994, with the conclusion of the Uruguay Round of GATT Multilateral Negotiations, the World Trade Organisation (WTO) was created. The Agreement Establishing the WTO included a range of limited provisions (11) on various cross-border competition issues.

▸ Substance and practice of competition law varies from jurisdiction to jurisdiction

It has many objectives:

- Protecting the interests of consumers (consumer welfare);
- Ensuring that entrepreneurs have an opportunity to compete in the market economy;
- Laws on deregulation (12) of access to markets;
- State aids and subsidies;
- The privatization of state-owned (13) assets;
- The establishment of independent sector regulators.
- Providing better public services.

NB: It has been argued that competition laws can produce adverse (14) effects when they reduce competition by protecting inefficient competitors and when costs of legal intervention are greater than benefits for the consumers.

▸ Intellectual property and competition have become increasingly intertwined (15)

On the one hand, it is believed that promotion of innovation through enforcement of intellectual rights promotes competitiveness (16), while on the other the contrary may be the consequence. The question rests on whether it is legal to acquire monopoly through accumulation of intellectual property. In which case, the judgment needs to decide between giving preference to intellectual rights (17) or towards promoting competitiveness:

- Should antitrust laws accord special treatment to intellectual property?
- Should intellectual rights be revoked (18) or not granted when antitrust laws are violated (19)?

Various anti-competitive effects and consequences due to:

– Intellectual properties that are collaboratively designed with consequence of violating antitrust laws (intentionally or otherwise);

– and the further effects on competition when such properties are accepted into industry standards;

– Cross-licensing of intellectual property;

– Bundling (20) of intellectual rights to long term business transactions or agreements to extend the market exclusiveness of intellectual rights beyond their statutory duration (21).

– Trade secrets (22), if they remain undecipherable (23), have an eternal length of life.

1. *competition* : concurrence
2. *conduct* : conduite, comportement
3. *guild* : guilde, corporation
4. *regulation* : contrôle, réglementention
5. *enforcement* : mise en vigueur
6. *completion* : achèvement
7. *collusion* : connivence
8. *abuse* : abus
9. *joint venture* : société en participation

10. *state aid* : aide – *subsidy* : subvention
11. *provision* : disposition
12. *deregulation* : déréglementation
13. *state-owned* : nationalisé
14. *adverse* : contraire
15. *intertwined* : entrelacé
16. *competitiveness* : compétitivité
17. *rights* : droits
18. *to revoke* : annuler, abroger
19. *to violate* : enfreindre, bafouer, violer
20. *bundling selling* : vente par lots
21. *statutory duration* : durée légale
22. *trade secrets* : secrets de fabrication
23. *undecipherable* : indéchiffrable

2 Zooming on

The high price of free accounts

The competition watchdog's challenge may be more bark than bite

AMID the gloom of a faltering economy and a slumping housing market, Britain's banks, with their supervisors in hot pursuit, have been stumbling from one crisis to another. Having written off billions of pounds on the value of exotic credit products, and then tapped shareholders for billions more to rebuild strained balance sheets, banks have been bracing themselves for the next shoe to drop.

Most expected it to come in the form of write-downs on bad loans in their traditional banking business. Some analysts reckon these may total as much as £19 billion, if defaults rise to levels last seen in the previous downturn in the early 1990s. Yet trouble, as so often happens, has come from an unexpected direction.

The Office of Fair Trading (OFT), a consumer-and-competition watchdog, has spent over a year examining the market for current accounts. In a report published on July 16th the OFT said that the system lacks transparency and does not serve consumers. This stark finding is likely to trigger changes that may slash the profitability of the most lucrative bit of British retail banking at a time that banks need every penny they can get.

Although Britain's system of free current accounts for customers who keep them in credit has long been popular, it comes at a hefty price. The OFT reckons that in 2006 British banks raked in £8.3 billion from supposedly free current accounts, worth 31% of their total revenue from retail banking. Current accounts were a bigger source of income than mortgage lending (19%), credit cards (13%) and savings accounts (17%).

For consumers, the biggest cost arises from the paltry rates of interest that banks pay on balances held in current accounts, usually less than 0.5%, which compares with rates of 5% or 6% now available on savings accounts. This hidden fee totals £4.1 billion a year. Another £2.6 billion or so comes from the charges paid by customers who exceed their credit limits.

The OFT dislikes these arrangements for a number of reasons. It frets about cross-subsidies, saying that the burden of fees for exceeding credit limits falls on the young and the poor, who are in effect padding the accounts of the rich (and, although it does not say so, the careful). And by obscuring the costs of services that customers might use more sparingly if they had to pay a fee –withdrawing cash, for instance – cross-subsidies may be driving up expenses for all customers.

The OFT also worries that there is less competition between banks than there might be if the costs of accounts were more readily apparent to consumers. That too may drive up the burden of banking for all.

The OFT may have identified a problem in the retail-banking market but it has been reticent about proposing solutions. Instead, it wants banks to come forward with ideas for making current accounts more transparent. It hopes that by coming clean on what the accounts cost, banks will have to offer better deals to customers, who will be empowered to shop around more. At present only 6% of British customers change banks in any year, a far lower rate of switching than in many other industries – almost half of households switched electricity suppliers, for instance, in 2005.

But the OFT's hopes for the redemptive power of transparency may be unrealistic for two reasons, both mentioned in its own report. The first is that most customers choose a bank based on how close its nearest branch is and only a small minority consider the bank's charges. Another is that most people paying fees for exceeding their credit limits usually know what the charge is. Although only a quarter of customers go overdrawn each year, most of these had also done so the previous year and were more likely to do so six times a year than just once. Transparency may help cut costs, but only if customers take full advantage of it.

The Economist print edition, July 17th, 2008

Personal current accounts in the UK

An Office of Fair Trading study

Key findings

The OFT has found evidence of competition in the Personal Current accounts (PCA) markets. Banks can also demonstrate high consumer satisfaction and low fees on many more visible elements of current accounts- such as withdrawals from ATMs (Automated Teller Machines). Internet and telephone banking have also made it easier for consumers to manage their account.

However, the OFT believes that the PCA market as a whole is not working well for consumers. A combination of complexity and a lack of transparency mean that consumers and competition are focused almost exclusively on more visible fees, and not on the less visible elements such as insufficient funds charges and foregone interest – despite the fact that these make up the vast bulk of banks' revenues. For insufficient funds charges, this effect is exacerbated by a lack of simple mechanisms for consumers to control, or opt out of an unarranged overdraft.

Furthermore, a significant proportion of consumers believe that it is complex and risky to switch accounts, with the result that switching rates are very low.

As a result, we believe the ability for the market to function well has become distorted in three ways:

First, there seems to be a substantial cross subsidisation from those consumers who incur insufficient funds charges to those who do not; and to a significant extent from 'vulnerable' low income and low saving consumers, to higher income, higher saving ones

Second, the extent of this cross subsidisation means there is a substantial misalignment between the banks' revenues and their costs on many of their products and services. This may lead to inefficiency through under or over consumption of services by consumers, and

Third, the lack of consumer awareness and switching on the less visible elements provides banks with little incentive to compete on them. This may also have an impact on longer term productivity within the banking sector. Without competition in these areas, banks have lower incentives to create new and innovative services.

Furthermore, given the constraints on competition, and in particular the low switching rates, we are not persuaded that any additional profits made from less visible elements are fully competed away in terms of lower fees in other areas. This raises the possibility that a significant proportion of the profits made on less visible elements are kept by banks rather than passed back to consumers through more intensive competition.

In essence, the OFT believes that the market may be stuck in an equilibrium that does not work well for many consumers. A significant number of consumers do not know how much they will effectively pay in bank fees or how individual elements in the charging structure will be implemented, either before or after they are incurred. This limited understanding of key account elements, combined with low confidence in switching, means that the banks have less incentive to provide better offers on insufficient funds charges and interest. Without better offers from banks, however, consumers have little incentive to switch

Share of retail banking revenue, 2006

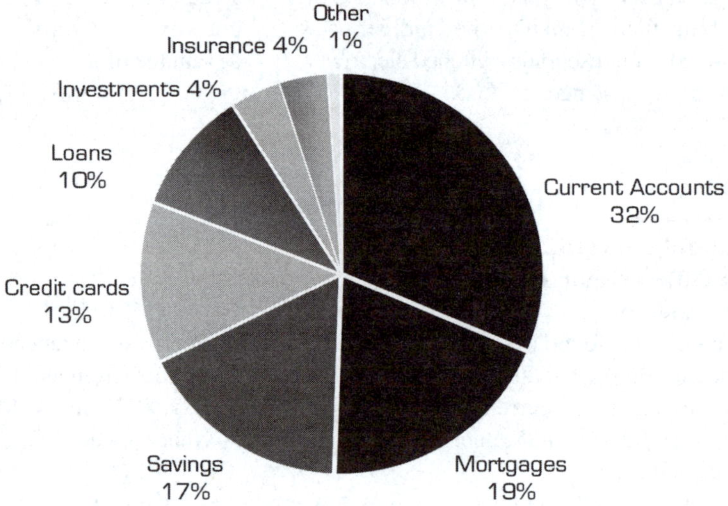

Break-down of PCA revenue (in millions), 2006

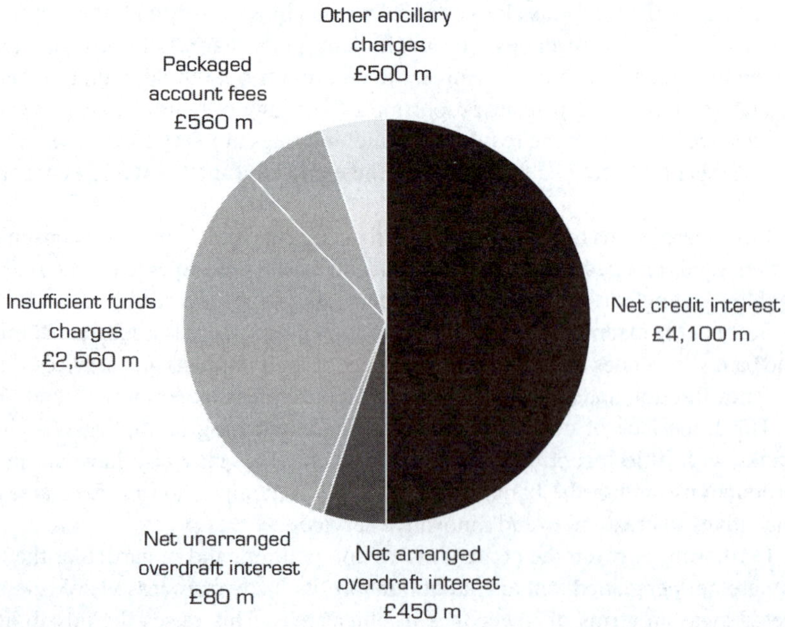

Challenger and four established bank market share by number of account customers, 1999-2007

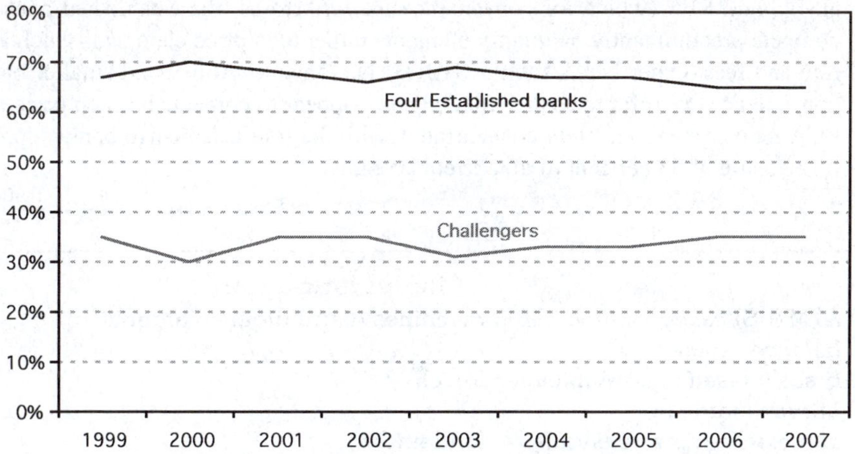

Credit interest rates, January 1993 – January 2008

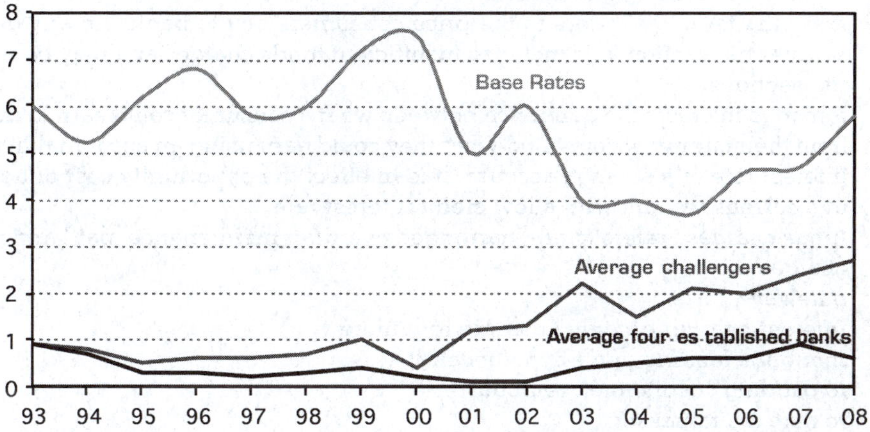

Personal current accounts

The personal current account is a cornerstone of Britain's retail finance system. Its efficient operation is essential for consumers.

A current account is used on a regular basis by 90 per cent of consumers. The UK PCA market is large. There are approximately 64 million accounts in the UK, of which 54 million are estimated to be active. Banks see PCAs as a gateway to selling other products. Consumers often select additional financial products from a bank with whom they have an existing relationship, without shopping around.

Furthermore, current accounts act as a gateway to financial inclusion for more vulnerable consumers. The main banks all offer basic bank accounts, which are particularly helpful for the financially vulnerable.

The most common account model in the UK is the so-called free-if-in-credit model. This model has a cost for consumers, which is not always apparent to them, in the form of interest forgone. This is the interest that consumers could earn by holding their credit balances in interest-bearing, or higher interest rate, accounts rather than leaving them in a current account that generally pays no, or only a minimal, interest on credit balances.

Broadly, the PCA market can be characterised by two types of competitors. Barclays, Lloyds, HSBC and RBS (which for convenience we refer to as 'the established banks' all appear to compete predominantly on quality elements rather than price elements – such as credit interest rate and fees. Other banks such as HBOS, Nationwide, Abbey and smaller banks (which, for convenience, we refer to as the 'challengers', appear to compete both on price and quality. The PCA industry is moderately concentrated, with the four established banks representing a combined share of 65 per cent of all current accounts.

Useful language

ATM (US)/*cash machine* (GB) : machines distributeurs d'argent.
balance : solde
brace oneself : rassembler ses forces
burden : fardeau
cornerstone : pierre angulaire, fondement
cross-subsidies : subventions croisées
defaults : défauts de paiement
to drive up : faire augmenter
fees : the term 'fee' refers to the price consumers pay to banks for any given current account transaction, this includes insufficient funds charges and may be zero for some transactions.
foregone interest : the difference between what a consumer could earn in credit interest from their current account and what they could earn using an account that pays higher interest rate or a savings account. It is in effect the opportunity cost of holding credit in a current account with a low credit interest rate.
funds charges : refers to an unarranged overdraft maintenance, paid and unpaid item charges.
gateway : porte
interest-bearing account : compte rémunéré
mortgage lending : prêt hypothécaire
to padding : capitonner, rembourrer
to rake in : ramasser
switch accounts : where customers face difficulties in switching between suppliers, whether because of monetary cost, administrative hurdles or just plain inconvenience, competition can be adversely affected. We refer to these as 'switching costs'.
to tap : soutirer
write-downs : dépréciations

3 Comprehension of documents

Exercice 9.1

Complétez le résumé avec les mots listés ci-dessous.

a. £2.6bn

b. regulation

c. transparency

d. uncompetitive
e. dominance
f. 54m
g. unable
h. subsidise
i. £8.3bn
j. incur
k. lack
l. risky
m. credit crunch
n. combined
o. cornerstone
p. work well
q. unaware
r. 0.5%
s. incentives
t. interest on customer's deposits

In 2006, the Office of Fair Trading estimated that in total, banks earned .... in revenues from Britain's .... active personal current accounts every year – more than they make from credit cards and savings accounts ....

The OFT threatened banks with greater .... and a full-blown investigation. That gives the lie to any claim that current accounts are free. In a hard-hitting report on the ....of the retail finance system, the consumer watchdog found that currently, customers paying charges for unauthorised overdrafts .... free banking for those in credit and that customers are .... of the charges they face.

Banks make .... from customers having insufficient funds on their accounts, often the result of simple customer mistakes. The banks make a further £4.1bn from ....

Releasing its report at a time when the banking industry is under intense pressure from the .... the OFT argued that the market does not ".......................... for consumers".

The watchdog's main areas of concern are:
– low level of .... on overdraft fees;
– complexity of charges;
– customers are .... to control whether they use services for which they pay;
– a significant proportion of customers consistently .... charges;
– a perception that switching accounts is complex and ....

Even customers who do not pay overdraft fees are losing out on interest payments on accounts in credit. In 2006, 88% of customers received interest of less than .... a year from current accounts. Free banking in the UK is a myth. The market is .... Customers .... the information they need to choose better deals, and this in turn weakens the banks' .... to compete for customers.

Despite the growing competition, the continuing .... of the "big four" proves the old adage that the British are more likely to change their partners than their current account provider.

Exercice 9.2

Certaines de ces affirmations sont fausses. Utilisez les informations fournies par les documents précédents pour les corriger.

1. Revenue from PCAs is largely generated through five sources: net interest income, debit interest (from arranged or unarranged overdrafts), insufficient funds charges, packaged fees and ancillary charges.
2. Around half of all revenue generated by accounts derives from insufficient funds charges.
3. In 2006, the aggregate revenue of banks from current accounts was approximately £3.8 billion.
4. The OFT survey states that banks are so lucrative because they charge customers whopping fees for basic services: bounced cheques, unarranged overdrafts, withdrawal from foreign cash machines.
5. The bulk of consumers pay a lot of attention to even basic details of their accounts.
6. Banks are accused of profiting from the financial difficulties of customers.
7. The big four banks continue to offer high rates to most customers.
8. The big four don't account anymore for the majority of the market.
9. The relative market shares of the established four and of the challenger banks were almost unchanged in 2007 compared with 1999.
10. More significantly, there has not been a marked difference in recent years between rates offered by the four established banks and those offered by the challengers.

4 Practice your technical skills

Exercice 9.3

La traduction

Traduisez en anglais.

1. En 2007 il y a eu une augmentation rapide du chômage de 3 %.
2. Le nombre de travailleurs du secteur bancaire a chuté de manière spectaculaire de 25 000 à 18 000 entre 2006 et 2008.
3. Le nombre d'actions négociées à la bourse s'est accru de 15 millions entre novembre et décembre.
4. Les exportations de produits chimiques sont restées stables au cours des deux dernières années,
5. Les chiffres ont diminué légèrement jusqu'à environ 650 millions en 2005 et se sont stabilisés à ce niveau jusqu'à 2007.
6. La société est sortie du rouge il ya deux ans ensuite il y a eu une amélioration importante des bénéfices chaque année pendant trois ans.
7. La société a fait une perte importante de 5 milliards de livres en 2006, après laquelle il y a eu une forte reprise.
8. Les ventes ont baissé de 25% pendant un an, et puis elles sont encore descendues deux fois.

Exercice 9.4

Remplacez *noms* **+** *adjectifs* **par** *verbes* **+** *adverbes***.**

Exemples :

1. Our prices have slightly increased recently. > **There was a slight increase in our prices.**
2. There was a gradual rise in sales in the last quarter. > **Sales rose gradually in the last quarter.**

1. The price increase led to a dramatic slump in sales.
2. The steel production progressed steadily until March.
3. After a well-conducted TV advertising campaign sales kept booming.
4. European carmakers are likely to lose market share significantly.
5. Japan's domestic market may grow fractionally by 1-2% a year.
6. After three years of rapid improvement, sales began to level off.

FICHE 10

La création d'entreprise

1 Ground work

Setting up a company

▸ Setting up a private company

The simplest form of business is the individual proprietorship or sole trader (1): for instance, a shop or a taxi owned by a single person. If several individuals wish to go into business together they can form a **partnership**; partners generally contribute equal capital, have equal authority in management, and share profits or losses. In many countries, doctors, lawyers and accountants are not allowed to form companies, but only partnerships with unlimited liability for debts, which should make them act responsibly.

A partnership is not a legal entity separate from its owners; like sole traders, partners have unlimited liability (2) for debts: in the case of bankruptcy, a partner with a personal fortune can lose it all. As a consequence, most businesses are limited companies (3) (US corporations, in which investors are only liable for the amount of capital they have invested. If a limited company goes bankrupt, its assets (4) are liquidated (5) to pay the debts; if the assets do not cover the debts, they remain unpaid i.e. creditors do not get their money back.

In Britain, most smaller enterprises are **private limited companies**. There are around one million. They usually have 'limited' or 'Ltd' at the end of their name and cannot offer shares to the public; their owners can only raise capital from friends or from banks and other venture capital (6) institutions.

A successful, growing British business can apply to the Stock Exchange (7) to become a **public limited company** (PLC). If accepted, it can publish a prospectus (8) and offer its shares for sale on the open market. There are about 2,000 in Britain; they have 'plc' at the end of their name. In The USA, there is no legal distinction between private and public corporations, the American equivalent of a PLC is a company or corporation registered with the Securities and Exchange Commission (SEC), also called a **listed company**. It has to make quarterly reports on:
- Sales revenue or turnover – the money received by the company in that period from selling goods or services
- Gross profit – turnover less cost of sales
- Net profit – gross profit less administrative expenses and tax

Companies on the London Stock Exchange, called **quoted companies**, have to produce a half-yearly interim report which informs shareholders about the company's progress. All companies with shareholders have to send them an **Annual Report** each financial year. This contains a review of the year's activity, and an examination of the company's financial position and results. There are also financial statements and notes and the auditor's report on the financial statements.

Public companies have to hold an **Annual General Meeting** AGM (in the US Annual meeting of stockholders) and so do most private ones. At this meeting the shareholders are informed about the content of the Annual report and the financial statements, they vote to accept or reject the dividend recommended by the directors, and vote on replacements for retiring (9) members of the board.

▸ Founding companies

When people start a company they have to draw up **Articles of Association** (in the US, bylaws), which set out:
- the rights and duties (10) of directors and shareholders
- different classes of shareholders
- and a **Memorandum of Association** (in the US, a Certificate of Incorporation), which states:
- the company's name
- the company's purpose – its objectives
- the company's registered office – where to send official documents
- the company's premises – Premises (always with an 's' at the end) is the technical term for the place in which a company does its business: a shop, a workshop, a factory, a warehouse, an office, etc.
- and authorised share capital – the maximum amount of a particular type of share the company can issue.

Companies' memoranda (11), articles of association and annual financial statements are sent to the registrar of companies, where they may be inspected by the public. A company that files (12) its financial statements late is almost certainly in trouble.

1. *sole trader* : the equivalent of the French 'entreprise individuelle' or EURL
2. *liability* : responsabilité
3. *limited company* : the equivalent of the French SARL
4. *assets* : actifs
5. *liquidated* : sold
6. *venture capital* : capital risque
7. *Stock Exchange* : bourse
8. *prospectus* : appel à souscription publique
9. *retiring* : qui prennent leur retraite
10. *rights and duties* : les droits et les devoirs
11. *memoranda* : pluriel de memorendum (cf datum/data)
12. *to file* : déposer

2 Zooming on

Lending Plan Won Prize, but Will It Work Here?

The maroon couch was big enough to take up half the living room, but by the time the 10th woman arrived it could hold no more.
Grameen America, in Queens, is the international organization's first United States venture. Since January, its loans have exceeded $250,000, in amounts ranging from $500 to $3,000.
The room temperature was rising from all the body heat. Chairs were brought in from the kitchen. Even the floor was called into service.

"I'd like to start the collection," Alethia Mendez announced after the last of the 15 women had arrived on a recent Saturday morning.
Therese Prentice counted out crisp bills, divided them, tucked them in envelopes and recorded the amount in a flimsy green book. The next woman repeated the exercise, until all 15 had made their payments for the week. Then the money was handed to Ms. Mendez, the group's 24-year-old banker.

"This is the way it was done in Bangladesh, so we do the same thing here," Ms. Prentice said. "It's our ritual."

The women are clients of Grameen Bank, the international organization that pioneered "microloans" to third-world entrepreneurs and that, along with its founder, won the Nobel Peace Prize in 2006.

But the women were not in one of the abjectly poor villages in Bangladesh where Grameen usually does business; they were in a modest two-story brick house in St. Albans, Queens.

Since the beginning of January, 11 Grameen lending groups have sprung up throughout Queens in the bank's first venture in the United States. They have lent more than $250,000, in amounts ranging from $500 to $3,000, to more than 100 women for income-generating activity like elder care, house-cleaning and flower-arranging businesses.

"Of the entire U.S. population, 40 percent is underbanked, and as a result end up using payday lenders, check cashers and other, more expensive services," said Vidar Jorgensen, president of Grameen America. "We're here to meet this huge need."

If the program works well, Grameen intends to expand nationwide. But while it has flourished elsewhere, it is not clear whether Grameen's model – which relies on peer pressure rather than collateral to make sure women repay their debts – will work here, and whether such small loans can actually help lift its borrowers out of poverty.

"In parts of the United States it may very well work, but I have real doubts about it working in places like New York City," said David R. Jones, president and chief executive officer of the Community Service Society of New York.

His group gives cash grants averaging $3,000 to city residents in financial distress – for instance, to people who have fallen behind on their rent or who cannot pay their medical bills. But Mr. Jones said that $3,000 is generally not enough to stabilize a New York resident.

Still, Grameen's experiment here is being closely watched. Elaine L. Edgcomb of the Aspen Institute in Washington, who co-wrote a 2005 study of more than 100 microlending programs in the United States, said that borrowers do "move out of poverty, and the business can be an important contributor to that, but it's not always the only contributor."

"For many families, the increase in income is sufficient to take them above the poverty line," she said.

Grameen's distinguishing feature is its mandatory weekly meetings at which borrowers learn money management skills from their banker and from one another and must make their payments in front of everyone else in the group. If one person defaults on a loan, Grameen will not call a lawyer or a collection agency or confiscate any assets. Instead, no one in the group will be eligible for a new loan.

"You have 30 eyeballs who are looking at you and making you accountable," said Myriam Pericles, a 41-year-old first-generation Haitian-American, who will use her $3,000 loan to expand her computer consulting business. She was a little skeptical about the process. "Maybe all this works in Bangladesh, but this is America, where people are different – our value system gets warped, our word is not our bond."

Nicole Brown, 30, who immigrated from Jamaica as a child, is using her $2,000 loan to start a day care business. "I didn't have it in my head to start my own business, but if you want to be great in life, you have to have your own stuff," she said. She added that she was drawn to Grameen through her sister, Wendy Brown, who is using her $3,000 loan to expand her apartment-cleaning business, Meticulous Cleaning Service L.L.C.

As the other group members looked on, Wendy Brown, 36, made her first payment on the $3,000 loan: $60 toward principal, $6 for interest and $2 toward a savings account. If she makes all her payments, she will retire the debt within a year and be eligible for another loan. "It's very simple, as opposed to getting it through a normal bank and going through the red tape and getting denied," she said.

Grameen America's managers, who are based in Jackson Heights, say that all the women in Queens are paying back their loans on time. But adapting its model to the United States has not been easy.

While Grameen officially requires a home visit to verify that borrowers are truly poor – they must fall below the United States Census Bureau's poverty line, currently defined as $21,027 for a four-person household with two children – some borrowers at the St. Albans meeting still had not received a visit. Grameen organizers said last week that all borrowers would receive home visits in the next few weeks.

Finding potential borrowers has been another challenge.

"Here, the women are not working in the community where they are living," said Shah Newaz, the general manager of the Jackson Heights office, who has worked with Grameen for 26 years all over the world. It is hard to meet with the women "because they are not in their houses in the daytime, and in the evening they are very tired and preparing meals, taking care of children and getting ready for the next day."

Grameen aims its loans at women, saying it has found them more responsible than men and more comfortable with the group model. So far, the Queens operation has lent only to women.

But the organization says it will lend to men here, and is aware that it cannot discriminate on the basis of gender. "We want a female candidate, but in the U.S. you can't say that in advertisements," Mr. Newaz said. "That is a problem."

The idea behind Grameen Bank began in Bangladesh in 1976, when Muhammad Yunus, an economics professor, lent a total of $27 to a group of 42 women in Jobra, a southern village. All of the women repaid their loans. Since 1983, when Mr. Yunus formally founded Grameen, it has lent $6.8 billion to 7.4 million Bangladeshis; 97 percent of its borrowers are women.

Mr. Yunus tried to start a microlending program in the United States in 1985, when he was invited to rural southern Arkansas by Bill Clinton, who was then the governor. But the program Mr. Yunus helped start, called the Good Faith Fund, failed. The group lending model never caught on. If given the choice, "any human being on earth would want to borrow as an individual rather than as a group member. It didn't work very well in this country," explained Mary Houghton, founder of ShoreBank, who helped advise the Arkansas experiment.

Another microfinance organization, Acción USA, which has lent money to more than 20,000 people since 1991, also attempted the group lending model in its early days. "We found that the group methodology did not work well because there was a general lack of trust among potential borrowers and an unwillingness to guarantee another person's loan," said Bill Burrus, president and chief executive of Acción USA. The organization has since adopted a more traditional individual lending model in almost all cases, and its default rate has ranged from 4 to 7 percent in recent years. Grameen says its default rate in Bangladesh was less than 1 percent, though higher in times of flooding.

Grameen America is aiming to reach 21,000 borrowers within five years, the number that its organizers say would allow it to break even. To improve its chances of success, it relies upon dense social networks, the kind often found in immigrant communities, to help form its groups of borrowers. The center in St. Albans consists predominantly of Caribbean and African-American women.

Not long ago, they would wait out winter afternoons between cleaning jobs on subway platforms, unable to afford lunch or dinner.

"We'd starve until we got home," Nicole Brown said. The sisters, who had moved back in with their mother, did not want to ask for more help from her, so they turned to Grameen.

"Last year, I had $3 in my pocket," Wendy Brown said. "This loan could help be the turning point."

The New York Times,
April 1st, 2008,
by Amanda M. Fairbanks

Useful language

to afford : se permettre financièrement, avoir les moyens de
ATM (*Automatic teller machine*) : DAB (distributeur automatique de billets)
bank account : compte (en banque)
bank payment : virement bancaire
barter : faire du troc
to be in the red : être dans le rouge
to build people's loyalty : construire la fidélité des gens
cash : liquide
change : monnaie
checkout : caisse de sortie
cheque (GB)/*check* (US) : chèque
chip : puce
to collect personal data : rassembler des données privées
convenient : pratique
credit card : carte de crédit
to cross-link : croiser des fichiers
currency : monnaie, devise
database : banque de données
fees : frais, coûts
to fill out profiles : remplir des fiches de renseignement
to fit : ajuster
to get into debt : s'endetter
to grant a privilege : accorder un privilège
to live below the poverty line : vivre au-dessous du seuil de pauvreté
to live beyond one's means : vivre au-dessus des ses moyens
to live on credit : vivre à crédit
to lure customers : attirer des clients
means of payment : moyens de paiement
meet customers' expectations : répondre aux attentes des consommateurs
to own : posséder
to pay cash : payer en liquide
to personalize the offer : personnaliser l'offre
PIN (personal identification number) : code secret
procedures : démarches
purchase : achat
to purchase/to buy : acheter
purse : porte-monnaie
recipient : bénéficiaire
to record : enregistrer
red tape : paperasserie
to reduce : réduire
to register : enregistrer
safe : sans danger
smart card : carte à puce
to spy on somebody : espionner quelqu'un
tailormade product : produit sur mesure
to track : suivre à la trace
wages/salary : salaire
wallet : portefeuille
to withdraw : retirer de l'argent

3 Comprehension of document

Exercice 10.1

Donnez les mots correspondant aux définitions.

1. somebody who gets a loan
2. a machine that gives you money
3. what is paid to you when you work
4. to attract customers
5. to complete forms with personal data

Exercice 10.2

Traduisez en français.

1. Then the money was handed to Ms. Mendez, the group's 24-year-old banker.
2. The women are clients of Grameen Bank, the international organization that pioneered "microloans" to third-world entrepreneurs and that, along with its founder, won the Nobel Peace Prize in 2006.
3. But while it has flourished elsewhere, it is not clear whether Grameen's model – which relies on peer pressure rather than collateral to make sure women repay their debts – will work here, and whether such small loans can actually help lift its borrowers out of poverty.
4. Grameen's distinguishing feature is its mandatory weekly meetings at which borrowers learn money management skills from their banker and from one another and must make their payments in front of everyone else in the group.
5. Grameen aims its loans at women, saying it has found them more responsible than men and more comfortable with the group model. So far, the Queens operation has lent only to women. But the organization says it will lend to men here, and is aware that it cannot discriminate on the basis of gender.

FICHE 11

Méthode
Le commentaire de texte

Le commentaire de texte restitue le texte en ordonnant les idées essentielles qu'il exprime.

1 Quelles différences y a-t-il entre le résumé et le commentaire ?

A. La nature du document et la source

Contrairement au résumé qui ne comporte pas d'introduction, vous ferez apparaître dans le commentaire une introduction qui indique la nature du document ainsi que sa source (le nom de la source, le titre du document, l'auteur et la date de publication lorsqu'elle est mentionnée).
Dans cette introduction, vous indiquerez également le sujet (ou les sujets) du texte.
Voici une liste de mots ou d'expressions qui pourront vous être utiles lors de la rédaction de votre introduction.

Ce document est un article de *Newsweek*	*This document is an article from Newsweek.*
Ce texte est extrait de...	*This text is an excerpt from...*
Il est adapté d'un journal américain.	*It is adapted from an American newspaper.*
un quotidien/un hebdomadaire/un mensuel	*a daily/a weekly/a monthly*
C'est une interview de... par...	*It is an interview of... by*
C'est un schéma// un tableau// un camembert	*It's a diagram/a chart// a table// a pie chart*
C'est un dessin humoristique.	*It's a cartoon.*
Le titre de l'article est...	*The article is entitled*
Il a été publié dans... le...	*It was published in... on the...*
Il y a également un sous-titre.	*There is also a subtitle.*
Le sous-titre donne des indices sur le sujet.	*The subtitle gives clues to the topic.*
Ce texte est basé sur...	*This text is based on...*
Ce texte parle de	*This text deals with/is about...*
L'idée dominante est...	*The key issue is...*
Le sujet principal est...	*The main topic is...*

B. L'organisation

Le résumé suit (généralement) l'ordre du texte.
En ce qui concerne le commentaire, après avoir repéré les idées essentielles (certaines idées secondaires, données chiffrées ou exemples seront donc omis), il faut ordonner ces idées et faire un plan structuré. La chronologie du texte de départ n'est donc (généralement) pas suivie.
Quelques mots ou expressions qui pourront vous être utiles lors de la rédaction de votre développement :

1. Pour commencer

Tout d'abord	*First/firstly/first and foremost/first of all/in the first place/to begin with.../to start with...*

2. Pour développer un sujet

Deuxièmement	*Secondly*
Troisièmement	*Thirdly*
Ensuite	*Then/Next*
À première vue	*At first sight*
En fait	*As a matter of fact/in fact/in any case*
A la réflexion	*On second thoughts*
Effectivement	*Actually*
De toute façon	*Anyway*
Dans la plupart des cas	*In most cases*
À cet égard	*In this respect*
Dans une certaine mesure	*To some extent*
En ce qui concerne...	*As far as... is concerned*
D'un point de vue (+ adjective)	*From a (adjective) point of view*

3. Pour ajouter un élément

Outre	*In addition to*
D'ailleurs	*Besides*
En outre	*Furthermore*
De plus	*Moreover/what's more/on top of that*
Aussi	*As well/also/too*
De même	*Similarly*

4. Pour donner des exemples

Par exemple	*For instance/for example/such as/like*
C'est-à-dire	*Namely*
Surtout	*Above all*

C. Le point de vue

Le point de vue du résumé est celui de l'auteur, un point de vue objectif.

Le point de vue du commentaire est celui du lecteur et cela vous amènera donc à rédiger (en plus de l'introduction) une conclusion. Cette conclusion vous permettra, le cas échéant, d'apporter une conclusion sur le texte, d'émettre un jugement voire d'apporter un regard critique. Vous pouvez également rapporter la problématique du texte à un autre thème proche.

▸ **Pour conclure**

En conclusion	*To conclude/in conclusion/as a conclusion*
En bref	*In brief/in short/to put it in a nutshell*
Finalement	*At last/finally/last but not least*

2 Comment rédiger un commentaire de texte ?

A. La lecture du texte, le repérage des idées et leur organisation

Lisez le texte et surlignez les idées essentielles.
Réfléchissez à votre plan en fonction des idées dont vous aurez fait la liste.
Organisez ces idées selon une logique (par exemple, avantages ≠ inconvénients ; passé ≠ avenir ; causes ≠ conséquences...).

B. La rédaction du commentaire

Voici une liste de mots ou d'expressions qui pourront vous être utiles lors de la rédaction de votre commentaire.

1. Le texte

Ce texte commence par...	*The text starts/begins with...*
Il est centré sur...	*It concentrates on...*
L'idée dominante est...	*The key issue is...*
La question qui se pose	*The question that arises...*
On peut remarquer que...	*It can be noticed that*
On dit...	*It is said...*
Ce point est illustré par...	*This point is illustrated by...*
Ce qui prédomine...	*What prevails...*
Ce texte étudie le pour et le contre/les avantages et les inconvénients...	*This text shows the pros and cons/the advantages and the drawbacks/the advantages and the downsides...*
Ceci soulève le problème de...	*This raises the problem of...*
... est un problème d'actualité.	*... is a topic of current interest.*
Cette question suscite des réactions.	*This question arouses reactions.*

2. L'auteur

Le journaliste	fait remarquer…	*The reporter*	*points out…*
	montre…		*shows…*
	explique…		*explains…*
	avance…		*puts forward…*
	dépeint…		*depicts…*
	affirme que…		*claims that…*
	fait allusion à…		*alludes to…*
	aborde le problème de…		*tackles the problem of…*
	prend en compte…		*takes in to account…*
	fait un parallèle entre…		*makes a parallel between…*
	met en opposition… et…		*contrasts… and…*
	met en évidence…		*highlights…*
	souligne…		*underlines…*
	met l'accent sur…		*stresses…*
	insiste sur…		*emphasizes…*
	se concentre sur…		*focuses on…*
	a une vision approfondie de…		*has a deep insight into*
	remet en cause…		*questions…*
	dénonce…		*denounces…*
	défend l'idée que…		*advocates/supports/stands for…*
	fait un plaidoyer pour…/ contre…		*makes a plea for…/ against…*
	ne fait pas mention de…		*doesn't mention…*

3. Donner son opinion

Je pense	*I think/I guess/*
Ma première impression est que…	*My first impression is…*
J'ai le sentiment que…	*I feel as if…/ I have the feeling that…*
Rien ne prouve que…	*There is no evidence that…*
Il va sans dire que…	*It goes without saying that…*
On ne peut affirmer avec certitude que…	*It can't be taken for granted that…*
On ne peut s'empêcher de penser que…	*One can't help thinking…*
On ne peut nier que…	*There is no denying that…*
Les opinions sont partagées.	*Opinions may be divided.*
Certains pensent que… alors que d'autres…	*Some think that… though others…*
C'est une question controversée.	*It is a controversial issue.*
Le journaliste semble de parti-pris.	*The journalist seems biased.*
Cela me rappelle…	*This reminds me of…*
On ne peut pas prendre parti.	*We can't take sides.*
Je vois les choses de la même manière que lui.	*I see things eye to eye with him.*
Je suis tout à fait convaincu par…	*I am quite convinced by…*
On reconnaît généralement que…	*It is generally acknowledged that…*

Ce qui me frappe, c'est que...	*What strikes me is that...*
Je suis très frappé par...	*I am very much impressed by...*
Cela nous fait prendre (pleinement) conscience que...	*That makes us (fully) aware that...*
Je considère que c'est un point de vue optimiste/pessimiste/réaliste.	*I consider it as an optimistic/pessimistic/ realistic point of view.*
Je ne peux pas approuver ces idées.	*I can't approve of these ideas.*
Je suis d'accord avec...	*I agree with...*
Je ne peux pas être d'accord avec...	*I can't agree with...*
Ces affirmations sont sans valeur.	*These arguments are worthless.*

La relecture est bien sûr indispensable pour vérifier la qualité de votre expression. N'oubliez pas également d'indiquer le nombre de mots employés.

Exercice 11.1

Faites le commentaire du texte de la Fiche 10 *Lending Plan Won Prize, but Will It Work Here?* en français en 380 mots (+/– 10%).

FICHE 12 L'organisation de l'entreprise

1 Ground work

Business Organisation

Most companies have a hierarchical or pyramidal structure with a single person or a group of people at the top and a number of people below them at each successive level. A chain of command runs down the hierarchy, so that all employees know who their boss is, to whom they report (1), and whom their subordinates (2) are, to whom they can give instructions.

Some people in a company have an assistant who helps them and has no line of authority, and is not integrated into the chain of command.

Most companies are made up of three groups of people: the shareholders (3) – who provide capital –, the management (4) and the **work force**. The management structure of a typical company is shown in this organisation chart.

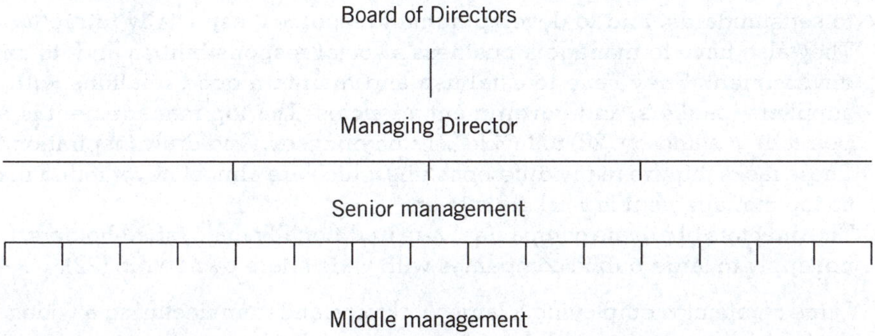

At the top of the company hierarchy is the Board of directors (5), headed by the Chairperson (6) or **President**. The board is responsible for policy decisions and strategy. It will usually appoint (7) a Managing Director (8) or **Chief Executive Officer**. **Senior managers** or **company officers** head the various departments or functions within the company, which may include the following:

A Marketing
B Public Relations (PR)
C Information Technology (IT)
D Personnel or Human Resources
E Finance
F Production
G Research and Development (R&D)

• Large British companies generally have a **chairperson** of the board of directors. He is in the driver's seat and oversees (9) operations. A group of people can very often produce better ideas and decisions than a single person working alone. The original idea is challenged, tested and modified by argument and discussion until it is improved and often transformed. The chairperson guides, stimulates and summarises the debate

– prevents it from becoming heated and turning into a clash of personalities. New and original suggestions are vital to the future development of any organisation and must be encouraged. It is up to the chairperson to persuade members of the board to turn suggestions into practical ideas.

• A **Managing Director** (MD) or **Chief Executive Officer** (CEO) is responsible for (10) the day-to-day running of the company and is supported (11) by various executive officers each with clearly defined authority and responsibility. (Marketing, PR, ICT, Personnel, Finance, Production, R&D). Management is essentially a matter of organising people. Managers divide the work into distinct activities and then into individual jobs. They select people to manage these activities and perform (12) the jobs. They have to be good at communication and motivation. They need to communicate the organisation's objectives to the people responsible for attaining (13) them. They have to motivate their staff to work well, to be productive, and to contribute something to the organisation. They make decisions about pay and promotion. They also have to measure the performance of their staff, and to ensure that the objectives are reached. Furthermore, they have to train (14) and develop their staff, so that their performance continues to improve.

Some managers obviously perform these tasks better than others. Most achievements (15) and failures (16) in business are the achievements and failures of individual managers.

• **Top managers** are appointed and dismissed (17) by a company's board of directors. They are supervised and advised (18) by the board. They have to set objectives (19) and develop strategies that will enable the company to achieve them. This will involve allocating the company's human, capital and physical resources. They are expected to set standards, and to develop human resources, especially future top managers. They also have to manage a business's social responsibilities and its impact on the environment. They have to establish and maintain good relations with customers, suppliers, bankers, and government agencies. The top management is naturally on permanent stand-by (20) to tackle (21) major crises. And draw inspiration from crises. These tasks require many different skills which are almost never found in one person, so top management is work for a team.

The directors of private companies were traditionally major shareholders, but this does not apply to large public companies with wide share ownership (22).

Large companies employing a large workforce and manufacturing a wide range of products have complex internal structures and normally decentralized into separate operating divisions, each with its own engineering, production and sales departments.

The activities of large companies are too elaborate to be organised in a single hierarchy, and require functional organisation, with production or operations, finance, marketing and personnel departments.

Inevitably with hierarchy, people at lower levels are unable to make important decisions, but are obliged to pass on responsibility (23) to their boss, unless responsibilities have been explicitly delegated. One solution to this problem is matrix management, in which employees report to more than one superior: the appropriate managers in the finance, manufacturing and sales departments.

Another idea is to have a network of teams instead of traditional departments, which are sometimes at war with each other; they are formed to carry out (24) a project, after which they are dissolved and their members reassigned (25). It is called a matrix structure.

• This is a fairly typical organisation for a manufacturing firm: it is divided into Finance, Production, Marketing, and Human Resources departments.

– **The Finance department** is composed of two sections: Financial Management, which is responsible for capital requirements, fund control, and credit, and Accounting.
– **The Production department** consists of five sections. The first of these is Production Control, which is in charge of both Scheduling and Materials Control. Then there is Purchasing, Manufacturing, Quality Control, and engineering Support. Manufacturing contains three sections: Tooling, Assembly, and Fabrication.
– **The Marketing department** is made up of three sections: Sales, Sales Promotion, and Advertising, whose heads are all accountable to the marketing manager.
– **The Human Resources department** is the simplest. It consists of two sections. One is responsible for recruitment and personnel matters, the other is in charge of training.

1. *to report to* : rendre compte à quelqu'un, être le subordonné de qqn (Le mot français report se traduit par *postponement*)
2. *subordinates* : subordonnés
3. *shareholders* : actionnaires
4. *management* : direction
5. *board of directors* : conseil d'administration
6. *chairperson* : Président du conseil d'administration
7. *to appoint somebody to a job* : nommer qqn
8. *Managing Director* : Directeur général
9. *to oversee* : superviser
10. *to be responsible for* : être responsable de
11. *to support sbdy* : soutenir qqn
12. *to perform a job/a task* : effectuer un travail
13. *to attain = to achieve = to reach objectives* : atteindre les objectifs
14. *to train* : former
15. *achievements* : réussites
16. *failures* : échecs
17. *to dismiss an employee* : renvoyer qqn
18. *to advise* : conseiller
19. *to set objectives* : fixer des objectifs
20. *permanent stand-by* : constamment sur le qui-vive
21. *to tackle, to deal with a problem* : résoudre un problème
22. *ownership* : la propriété, la possession
23. *pass on responsibility* : décliner la responsabilité
24. *to carry out* : effectuer, mener à bien
25. *reassigned* : reclassé

2 Zooming on

"It's probably not a good sign to be listed in the organization chart underneath the office plants."

3 Comprehension of document

Exercice 12.1

Complétez l'organigramme suivant en utilisant la dernière partie de la fiche *Business Organisation*.

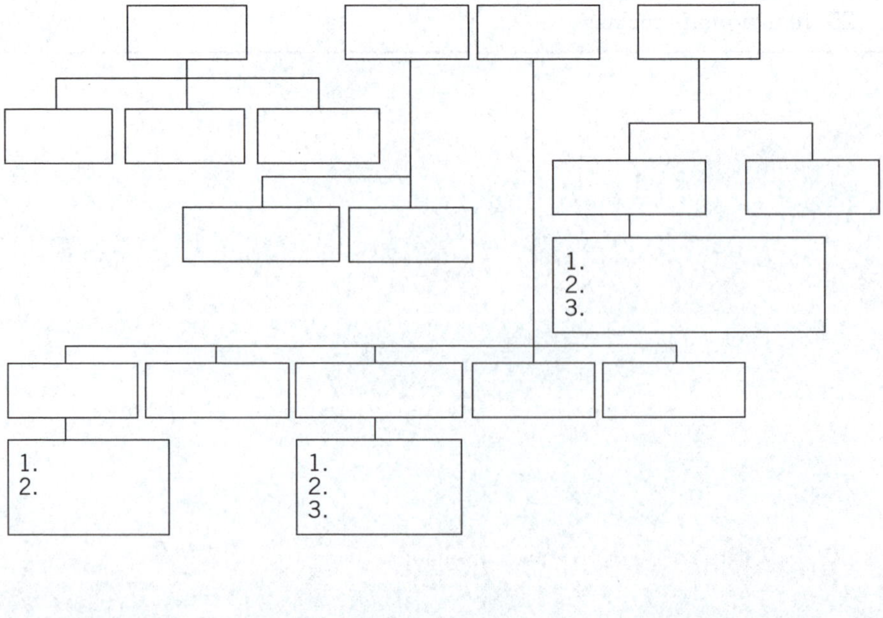

Exercice 12.2

Barrez les mots qui ne sont pas appropriés.

a. The organisation above is a *flat/hierarchical* structure.

b. The diagram shows a *traditional/innovative* structure.

c. The diagram represents a *matrix/functional* structure

d. The company is likely to be a *services/manufacturing* company

e. It is typical of a *small or medium-sized (SME)/large enterprise*.

f. The business is probably *complex/simple*.

FICHE 13

Méthode
La correspondance

Les emails ou courriels deviennent un outil essentiel dans les relations d'affaires. Ils ont un effet phénoménal sur notre manière de communiquer. Cependant l'explosion des emails est à l'origine de certains problèmes. Principalement du fait qu'il n'y a jamais eu de guide strict sur la façon de les utiliser. Aussi les systèmes informatiques sont-ils surchargés, les malentendus font des ravages et causent beaucoup de perte de temps.
De plus, le caractère apparemment informel des emails nous fait parfois aborder des sujets qu'on n'évoquerait pas dans une lettre d'affaires. Cela peut avoir des conséquences graves pour certaines entreprises, les conduisant parfois jusqu'au tribunal.
Les entreprises se rendent actuellement compte de l'importance de se protéger contre les dangers des emails. Pour une communication réellement efficace le moyen doit être adapté au message.

1 Les étapes de la rédaction d'une lettre commerciale en anglais

A. Les premiers éléments à indiquer

1. La référence

Elle comprend les initiales de l'expéditeur (généralement en majuscules) et de la personne qui tape (soit en majuscules, soit en minuscules). Une référence à un dossier ou à un service particulier peut aussi y figurer.

- **Exemple**

JB/TS   JB/ts/Per1   JB/TS/125

2. La date

Elle doit être écrite sans abréviations. Au Royaume-Uni, l'ordre des mots est Jour/Mois/Année, et il n'y a aucune virgule.

- **Exemple**

15 July 2008

3. L'adresse intérieure

Il faut taper le nom et l'adresse du destinataire sur des lignes séparées comme sur une enveloppe. On s'adresse à la personne qui signe « Mary Douglas » sous le même nom précédé du terme de courtoisie : Mrs/Ms. « Mrs M douglas » ne serait pas correct.

- **Exemple**

Mrs Mary Douglas
General Manager
Douglas Engineering Co Ltd
50 Molehill Road
Manchester
M60 7AS

4. Salutation

Si le nom du destinataire a été utilisé dans l'adresse intérieure, il est d'usage d'ouvrir par une salutation personnelle (sans virgule).

- **Exemple**

Dear Mr Clinton   Dear Mary   Dear Miss Sharp

Si votre lettre est adressée à un chef de service ou au directeur d'une entreprise dont le nom n'est pas connu, il serait plus approprié d'utiliser une salutation plus neutre.

- **Exemple**

Dear Sir or Madam

5. Objet

On le place sur la ligne suivant immédiatement la salutation, ce qui donne une brève indication du contenu de la lettre.

- **Exemple**

Dear Miss Sharp
NEW WORKING HOURS – 13 JUNE 2008

B. Le contenu de la lettre

1. Introduction

Le premier paragraphe indiquera la raison de la communication, son but est de cadrer ce qui suit :
– accuser réception de la correspondance précédente ;
– faire référence à une réunion ou à un contact ;
– fournir une entrée en matière au sujet qui va être discuté.

- **Exemple**

Thank you for your letter of...
It was good to meet you again at last month's conference.
We wish to hold our annual meeting at a Manchester hotel in October.

2. Corps de la lettre

Dans cette partie, le message livre toutes les informations dont le destinataire a besoin. Vous pouvez aussi demander des informations, parfois les deux cas cohabitent. Il faut vous exprimer simplement et le plus clairement possible dans des paragraphes bien séparés pour chaque cas. Cette partie doit logiquement mener à une conclusion naturelle.

3. Conclusion

Cette partie achève le message par une conclusion logique, soit :
– dire clairement l'attente que l'on a de la part du destinataire ;
– dire ce que vous allez faire suite aux informations fournies.

4. Formule de politesse

Elle sert à clore la lettre poliment.

- **Exemple**

Dear Sir Dear Sirs Dear Madam Dear Sir or Madam	Yours faithfully (sans virgule)
Dear Miss Sharp Dear Linda Dear Mohamed	Yours sincerely (sans virgule)

C. Les derniers éléments à indiquer

1. Nom et désignation de l'expéditeur

Après la formule de politesse, on laisse 4 ou 5 espaces libres pour permettre de signer la lettre. La désignation de l'expéditeur apparaît directement sous son nom. Le titre « Mr » n'apparaît pas lorsque l'expéditeur est un homme alors que, par courtoisie à l'égard d'une dame, on fait suivre son nom d'un titre entre parenthèses.

- **Exemple**

Yours faithfully	Yours sincerely
Andrew Child Chairman	*Shirley Bertram* (Mrs) General Manager

Quand une lettre doit être signée à la place de l'expéditeur, pour le directeur, la mention qui précède la signature du subordonné qui remplace cette personne est « for » ou « pp » (*per procurationem*), par procuration.

- **Exemple**

Your faithfully
Lesley Grant
For RUPPERT NIVEN
Chairman

2. Pièces jointes

Signalez-les en indiquant « Enc » ou « Encs » au bas de la lettre en laissant un espace après la désignation de l'expéditeur.

- **Exemple**

Yours sincerely
Emma Swanson
Marketing Manager (Mrs)
ENCS

D. Exemple de présentation

Voici un modèle de lettre de candidature (*application for a job*) :

adresse de l'expéditeur
Ms J. BRITTON
13 Melrose Mansions
London EC1 V1LE

adresse du destinataire
Mr W R Morland
Personnel Manager
News Magazine
Fleet Street Publications
19 Amber Street
London W1P 4AH

date
8 February 2008

salutation
Dear Mr Morland

objet
Application for Private Secretary to Managing Director

introduction
With reference to our advertisement in the News Magazine three days ago, I wish to apply for the position of private secretary to the Managing Director.

corps de la lettre
I am twenty seven years old and I am presently working as Private Secretary to the General Manager at a manufacturing company and have a wide range of responsibilities. These include attending and taking minutes of meetings and interviews, dealing with callers and correspondence in my employer's absence, and supervising junior staff, as well as the usual secretarial duties. Prior to this, I worked as a journalist on the motor magazine "Motors", hence my desire to return to the world of publishing.

The kind of work in which your company is engaged particularly interests me, and I would welcome the opportunity it would afford to use my language abilities which are not utilized in my present post.

conclusion
I enclose a copy of my curriculum vitae with copies of previous testimonials.
I hope to hear from you soon to be given the opportunity to present myself at an interview.

formule de politesse
Yours sincerely

Signature
J. Britton
Jean Britton (Miss)

pièces jointes
Encs

Exercice 13.1

Lisez les documents suivants et répondez aux questions.

1. Do all the documents have a letterhead?
2. When do you use the following courtesy titles Ms, Mrs, Miss when you write to a woman?
3. Which opening salutation do you use when you don't know the name of the person?
4. Which complimentary close do you use in a letter when you don't know the name of the person?

5. Which complimentary close do you use in a letter that begins with the receiver's name, e.g. Dear Ms Baker, Dear James, etc?
6. Which expression is sometimes used to a business associate before closing?
7. What do the following abbreviations mean?

a. encs
b. incl
c. asap
d. pp
e. no
f. plc
g. St
h. Rd

1

ETS MAGNUM
30, rue Sainte Catherine
33000 BORDEAUX

Ms Baker
Project Manager
Publishall Co Ltd
35 Broad Terrace
Leeds LS3 9HY
UK

10 December

Dear Ms Baker

Thank you for your letter of 22 November and for the obliging remarks you made concerning our company. I apologize for not replying sooner but I have just returned from holiday.

I would be delighted to act as consultant for the *Drink Wine in France* chapter in your new project. The project sounds most interesting and I will be pleased to help you in any way I can.

I am afraid I will not be able to meet you next Friday owing to my professional Commitments, but I will be available during the second week of February.

I enclose a copy of our catalogue, *A Taste of Bordeaux*, which I hope you will find useful.

I look forward to meeting you in February.

Yours sincerely

Jeanne Delmas
Jeanne Delmas (Mrs)

2

BTS
BRIGHT TRIPS SERVICES
23 Station Road
London WIM 2LH
Tel:0172 684 9704
Fax: 0172 685 44 33

Mr J. Crosthwaite
Sparks & Lights Ltd
30 Church Street
Uppingham
Leicestershire LE 15 8PY

30 April 2008

Dear James

Please find enclosed airline tickets for Ms L Bridges and Mr R Brown.

Would you kindly check the tickets to make sure all the bookings are as requested.

Unfortunately the hotel you requested in Granada is fully booked due to an international business show taking place at that time. I am awaiting confirmation of a booking at the Husa President

Please let me know if you require any information on hotels in Sevilla.

With best wishes

Yours sincerely

Betty Sharp

Betty Sharp

encs

3

To: Hotel Husa President, Granada — Date: 19 May
From: Betty Sharp — No. of pages to follow: 0

Could you please reserve two single rooms with bathroom for Ms L Bridges and Mr R Brown? They will be arriving on 28 May and leaving on the morning of 31 May. Please send confirmation of this booking. incl. exact cost. by return.

Regards

B Sharp

4

MEMO

TO: Liz — Date: 14 July
FROM: Yuri — Subject: PUBLISHALL Party

Had a really good time up the mountain. Nice of you to take me up. I'm o to Ireland for four days (back Tues). Could you check my list of people to invite to our 10 th anniversary celebration and add anyone else you think of. Shirley needs to send out invitations asap.

Yuri

5

RIDGEWAY POTTERY
15OldTuckStreet
BristolBS12BQ

O'SHEE
Pharmaceuticals plc
Human Resources Dept
29 Narrow Road
Birmingham B1 2HE

12 June

Dear Sir or Madam

You have previously supplied us with crockery and we should be glad if you would now quote for the items named bellow. The pattern we require is 'number 45 China bone (blue) gilt rimmed'.

200 Teacups and Saucer
200 Tea Plates
30 1-litre Teapots

We would appreciate if you could quote prices including packing and delivery to the above address. Please also state discounts allowable, terms of payment and earliest possible date of delivery.

Yours faithfully

T. Bailey

T Bailey
pp B Thomas
Human Resources Manager

6

PUBLISHALL CO LTD

28 January

Dear Mr Garcia

I was pleased to meet you in Sevilla last week. Mr Brown and I would like to thank you for a most interesting and informative visit, and for giving us so much of your time.

It was a pleasure that you have agreed to a further interview, for inclusion in our new project *Eat and Drink in Spain*. We will contact you shortly to finalize arrangements. Perhaps we can extend our interview over lunch.

Please give our kind regards to Mr Ortega.

Mr Brown and I very much look forward to meeting you again.

Yours sincerely

Lily Bridges

Lily Bridges
Project Director
Publishall Publications

Head Office: Publishall CO LTD, 35 Broad Terrace, Leeds LH3 9HY

2 L'écriture des emails

A. Les pièges à éviter

▸ **La date et l'heure**

En les fixant correctement, elles vous aident à garder la trace de vos messages.

▸ **Les objets**

Ils doivent être très courts et très clairs, et doivent annoncer exactement au lecteur ce qui va suivre dans le contenu du mail.

▸ **Les messages vagues**

Écrivez des messages spécifiques et compréhensibles. Prenez le temps de composer votre message avec soin et de trouver le ton juste. Usez de phrases et de paragraphes courts et reformuler succinctement les longues phrases.

▸ **Les fautes grammaticales, les messages bâclés ou les fautes d'orthographe**

Ils empêchent votre lecteur de comprendre les messages. La précipitation rendra vos messages abrupts, abrégés et truffés d'erreurs. Respectez votre lecteur. Assurez-vous que votre message est bref, clair et agréablement présenté.

▸ **CC à la terre entière**

C'est ce que font beaucoup de gens. Nous devons supporter des boites de réception qui débordent et une perte de temps énorme. Donc n'envoyez des exemplaires qu'à ceux qui ont vraiment besoin de savoir. Pas à tous ceux que vous connaissez.

B. Les conseils indispensables

• Écrivez un objet clair et bien adapté **après** avoir écrit votre message.

• Pensez à utiliser une salutation appropriée et une formule de clôture. Le caractère informel est toléré dans les emails. Quand vous contactez quelqu'un pour la première fois dans une société, il est d'usage de rester formel. Par la suite, on devient souvent plus détendu.

• **Exemple**

Remplacez « *Dear Sue* » par « *Hi Sue* », « *Yours sincerely* » par « *Best wishes* ».

• N'écrivez jamais tout en MAJUSCULES dans votre message. Même si vous voulez attirer l'attention. C'est comme si vous hurliez, ce qui n'est pas poli.

• Utilisez des phrases simples. Sauter des mots est courant dans les e-mails et le discours informel. Cela se produit entre gens qui se connaissent bien, et quand la situation est détendue et amicale, ou quand le sens du message reste clair grâce au contexte. Alors la forme grammaticale entière n'est pas nécessaire.

• **Exemple**

(That's a) good idea!
(I) think your idea is great.
(I) hope you are well.
(I am) looking forward to seeing you.
Flying via LA (would be) quicker.
His plans (are) uncertain.

(Did you) get my email?
(Are you) coming with us on Monday?
(It's a) pity we missed you yesterday.
Your idea (is) good, but needs clarification.
(Have you) sent the memo?
(I) told (the) staff about (the) merger.

Autres abréviations :

'c' = see	*'yr'* = your	*'asap'* = as soon as possible
Pls = please	*thx* = thanks	*rgds* = regards
re = with reference to	*i.e* = id est (c'est-à-dire)	*e.g.* = exempli gratia (par exemple)
NB = nota bene	*PS* = postscriptum	

On use aussi d'acronymes (les premières lettres des mots).

- **Exemple**

TIA = thanks in advance

BTW = by the way

FYI = for your information

BW = best wishes

Rappelez-vous que l'usage d'acronymes peut être considéré comme peu professionnel dans certaines situations, surtout si vous ne connaissez pas très bien le destinataire.

• Il est important de structurer logiquement vos messages. Faites usage des mots de liaison : *so*, *however*, *although*, *nevertheless*, *due to*, *as a result*, *despite*, *whereas*, *in conclusion*, *in fact*, *above all*, *furthermore*, etc.
• Numérotez vos lignes ou vos paragraphes à l'aide de numéros, de puces ou de sous-titres pour que votre message gagne en clarté.
• Formatez vos messages d'une manière agréable à lire, en laissant un espace entre chaque paragraphe.
• Écrivez comme si vous aviez une conversation avec une personne vivante à l'autre bout.
• Relisez-vous et assurez-vous que tout est correct **avant** de cliquer sur la touche « envoi ».

Exercice 13.2

Choisissez un des objets pour chaque mail. Un d'entre eux n'est pas utilisé.

a. Re your advertisement
b. Meeting 11/6
c. Shipping confirmation
d. Special Offer!
e. Regarding your order
f. Action re contract

Email 1
Subject: ...
Sorry for the delay in answering due to my absence from the office through illness. Unfortunately, the items you ordered are not in stock, but we are expecting delivery by the end of the week. I'll get back to you as soon as they arrive. If need any more information, please feel free to contact me.
Email 2
Subject: ...
Re your last email we are now arranging the meeting scheduled for 11 June, but there are still a few details I need from you. Do you want us to book hotel accommodation for you – or will you sort it out at your end? Also, can you send us information about London's project you

were involved in last Christmas? It would be helpful to have something to circulate before the meeting. Please send us a copy of any relevant reports. Regards, Mona.

Email 3

Subject: ...

Just a short note to let you know that we received your order. We can confirm that the items were sent by mail today. To track your order, click on the link below. If there's anything else, just let us know. Best wishes. Patrick.

Email 4

Subject: ...

Good news! Subscribers to our email newsletter can take advantage of fantastic price savings in our March sale. I've attached a pdf file that gives full details, or alternately just click on the link below. You can order over the web or by email – our customer service staff are standing by. Looking forward to hearing from you soon.

Email 5

Subject: ...

Meredith, I've emailed Alistair and Angus about the changes to the contract. Shall I have a word with Alistair to make sure he understands what's going on? You work with Angus – Can you talk to him? Thanks for your help – I appreciate.

L'objet du mail doit être très court et clair. Il doit annoncer au lecteur ce qu'il va trouver dans le corps du mail.

Exercice 13.3

Faites correspondre les expressions soulignées de l'exercice 13.2 avec celles ci-dessous.

Previous contact	
With reference to your email sent (date)...	1...... *Re your last email* ....
Reason for email	
We are writing to inform you that...	2 ....
Good news	
You will be pleased to hear...	3..
We are able to confirm that...	4 ....
Apologising/Bad news	
I apologise for...	5 ....
We regret to inform you that...	6 ....
Requests	
I'd be grateful if you could...	7 ....
I would appreciate it if you could...	8 ....
Offering help	
Would you like me to...	9 ....
If you wish, I would be happy to...	10 ....
Promising action	
I will contact you again...	11 ....
Attachments	
Please find attached...	12 ....
Final comments	
Thank you for your help	13 ....
Do not hesitate to contact us again	14 ....

Closing

We are looking forward to... 15 ....

Yours/Yours sincerely 16 ....

! *Les expressions de gauche sont plus formelles que celles de droite.*

Exercice 13.4

Lisez le courriel suivant et choisissez le mot qui convient dans chaque ligne (A, B, C...).

Pierre – Here's the summary of the market report for South America that I promised you. As we all know, last year was a difficult one. a).. since February things b).. been getting better. Sales have recovered c).. 4% in Chili, our biggest market. We are d).. to see a similar e).. in Venezuela and Peru over the next few quarters, f).. right now sales there are g)..

In relation to the long term, we are optimistic. Our h).. is that economic growth in the whole region i).. begin to j).. from the start of next year. This will k).. labour market and other structural reforms, which in our opinion will take place l)..;there are some changes in the government. This growth will m).. many new opportunities, n).. we will face increasing competition from US and other companies.

	1	2	3	4
A	so	even if	despite	however
B	have slow	have slowly	are slow	are slowly
C	for	with	by	on
D	possibility	perhaps	possible	likely
E	recover	improve	improvement	growing
F	although	nevertheless	so	as a result of
G	plain	equal	flat	level
H	trend	forecasting	prevision	forecast
I	will	shall	is going	it is possible
J	steady rise	rise steadily	rising steadily	will rise steadily
K	be due to	result of	be resulted from	because of
L	as a result	whereas	even if	despite
M	create	lead	result to	improve
N	despite	whereas	so	even though

Exercice 13.5

Trouvez dans la liste ci-après deux mots de liaison adaptés à chaque expression. Quels sont les deux mots de liaison qui ne sont jamais suivis d'une virgule et qui peuvent se trouver en milieu de phrase?

a. above all
b. therefore
c. as a result
d. even though
e. firstly
f. however
g. finally
h. taking everything into consideration
i. nevertheless
j furthermore
k in addition
l. in reality
m. in addition
n. in conclusion
o. in conclusion
p. in particular

Listing points	1	.... *Finally*	/ ....
Adding another point	2	....	/ ....
Making a contrast (but)	3	....	/ ....
Making a contrast (although)	4	....	/ ....
Giving the consequence (so)	5	....	/ ....
Giving the most important	6	....	/ ....
Saying what the situation really is	7	....	/ ....
Introducing the final paragraph	8	....	/ ....

Exercice 13.6

Remplacez les expressions lettrées (A-J) des emails par une des expressions moins formelles et plus courtes.

1. Don't forget
2. I can't make
3. I'm sorry to tell you
4. Re
5. Rgds
6. Can I
7. Feel free to
8. I have to
9. Can you
10. See you on Monday

Dear all
I would like to remind you (A) that we have a Board meeting on Monday at 10, as I told you last week. I've reserved the small conference room at the Marriott. You should receive the figures from Jane tomorrow morning. Don't hesitate to (B) request any further information you require.
I look forward to seeing you on Monday. (C)

Regards (D)
Evelyn

Dear Evelyn
With reference to your email (E), I regret to inform you (F) that I will not be able to attend (G) the Board meeting on Monday, as it is necessary for me (H) to go to head office for the day.
I would be grateful (I) if you could give us more notice in future, and inform us about meetings several days in advance.
I wonder if I could send (J) Clara to the meeting instead?

Regards
Ali

Exercice 13.7

Corrigez les erreurs dans chaque phrase.

1. Please send me your comments until Tuesday at the latest.
2. I will be grateful if you could send me more information.
3. I'm write with regard to your recent email.
4. Please find attach my report, as promised in Monday's meeting.
5. I am really appreciate your kindness during my stay in Manchester.
6. Can we meet at 15Apr at 12.30 instead?
7. If you require any further informations, please contact me.
8. I apologise the delay.
9. I look forward to hearing you soon.
10. It will be more better for me if we meet on Friday rather than Thursday.
11. I'm afraid but we haven't received your payment yet.
12. Please get back me if there's anything else.

Exercice 13.8

Vous êtes la porte parole de la BBA, the British Bankers' Association et vous envoyez un email aux membres principaux de votre association dans lequel vous commentez succinctement l'enquête de l'OFT.

From	Angela.Knight@BBA.co.UK
Date	07: 09: 08
To	Nicolas Freeman@Barclays plc.com
CC	All members
Subject	The OFT's survey

• Vous déplorez les critiques que cet organisme fait alors que le crédit connaît un moment critique (*credit crunch*) : trop grande complexité des comptes bancaires et accusations de dissimuler les frais encourus par les clients.
• L'OFT n'a regardé que les revenus des banques sans considérer le coût de la gestion d'un compte courant.
• Le marché bancaire est très compétitif et le chiffre annuel des frais est légèrement exagéré parce que l'enquête souligne quelque chose que nous ne cessons de répéter : 80% des clients ne paient pas de frais pour les services bancaires. Si les banques devaient changer les méthodes actuelles, d'autres frais seraient introduits.

• Vous ajoutez que le modèle bancaire actuel correspond à ce qu'ont demandé les clients et qu'il est important que demeure la gratuité pour les services bancaires normaux.
• La structure des frais bancaires est claire et évidente dans les courriers adressés aux clients.
• Les clients paient pour des transactions qui n'ont pas été prévues à l'avance, mais veulent-ils vraiment payer pour l'utilisation des distributeurs d'argent, pour les relevés bancaires (*statements*), ou les prélèvements automatiques (*direct debits*) dans ce pays ?
• Vous concluez en engageant le secteur bancaire à plus de transparence et surtout à faciliter les mouvements entre comptes.

Useful language for writing a letter of complaint

1. Opening the letter
"I'm sorry to tell you that…"
"I'm writing to complain about…"
"I'm writing with reference to…"
2. Explaining why you are dissatisfied
"There seems to have been an error."
"There appears to be a mistake/a misunderstanding."
3. Requesting action
"I would be glad if you would look into the matter."
4. Suggesting action
"The best solution would be to…"
"I'd like to suggest that…"

FICHE 14

L'analyse des performances de l'entreprise

1 Ground work

Accounting Policies and Standards

Companies are required by law to give their shareholders certain financial information so they have to publish the value of their assets and liabilities. Companies also have to calculate their profits and losses: their managers, shareholders, bondholders (1) and the tax authorities need this information.

Although companies can choose their way of doing their accounts: their **accounting policies**, they have to be consistent, which means regularly using the same method every year, unless there is a good reason to change a policy: this is the **consistency principle**.

The policies also have to be **disclosed** or made known to the shareholders: the Annual Report will contain a Statement of Accounting Policies that mentions any changes that have been made. There is a range of methods of valuation (2) – to decide how much something is worth – and measurement – to determine how big something is – that are accepted by law or by official accounting standards.

In the USA, there are Generally Accepted Accounting Principles (GAAP). In the rest of the world, there are International Financial Reporting Standards (IFRS). These are technical rules or **conventions** – accepted methods of doing things that are not written down in a law.

The choice of policies can make a big difference to the profit (3) figure depending on how they depreciated their assets (4) – **depreciation**: the process of converting (5) an asset into an expense –, depending on how valued their stock or inventory or if they made depreciation **provisions**. The accounts of British companies have to give **a true and fair view** of their financial situation.

▸ **The most important principles**

• The full-disclosure principle means that financial reporting must include all significant information.
• The principle of materiality, however, states that very small and unimportant amounts do not need to be shown.
• The principle of conservatism says that where different accounting methods are possible, you choose the method that is least likely to (6) over-estimate assets or income.
• The objectivity principle states that accounts should be based on facts and not on personal opinions or feelings. Accounts should therefore be verifiable. However, depreciation or amortization, and provisions for bad debts, for example, are necessarily subjective.
• The revenue recognition principle is that revenue is recognised in the accounting period in which it is earned (7) i.e. the revenue is recorded when a service is provided or goods delivered, not when they are paid for.

• The matching principle is related to revenue recognition and says each cost or expense related to revenue earned must be recorded in the same accounting period as the revenue it helped to earn.

▸ **Financial Statements**

• **The Profit and Loss account** (8) (UK) or the income statement (US) shows revenue and expenditure for a specific period. It gives figures for turnover (9) (UK) or net sales (US) – the amount of business done by the company during the year – and for costs of sales (UK) or cost of goods sold (US), and overheads (10). The first figure should be greater than the second: there should be a profit – an excess of income over expenditure (11). Gross profit (UK) or gross margin (US). Profit before taxes (UK) or pre-tax income (US). Part of the profit is paid to the government in taxation – tax on profit (UK) or income tax (US), part is usually distributed to shareholders as a dividend, and part is retained by the company to finance further growth (12) to repay debts, to allow for future losses, and so on. The EPS –Earnings per share (13) – are also indicated in the Profit and Loss Account, one of the most important measure of a company's strength. They represent the earnings returned on the initial investment amount. Obviously, the higher this number, the more money the company is making.
This ratio is calculated simply by dividing the company's net income by the number of shares outstanding (14) during the same period.

• **The balance sheet** (see following document)
• **The cash flow statement** (15), also known in financial accounting as statement of cash flows or funds flow statement (UK) or the statement of changes in financial position (US), is the third financial statement that shows how changes in balance sheet accounts and income affect cash and cash equivalents, and breaks the analysis down (16) to operating (17), investing, and financing activities. Essentially, the cash flow statement is concerned with the flow of cash in and cash out of the business. The statement captures (18) both the current operating results and the accompanying changes in the balance sheet. As an analytical tool (19), the statement of cash flows is useful in determining the short-term viability of a company, particularly its ability to pay bills (20). International Accounting Standard 7 (IAS 7), is the International Accounting Standard that deals with cash flow statements.
It includes trading profits (21), depreciation provisions, borrowing (22), the sale of assets, and the issuing of shares (23), the purchase of fixed or financial assets, the payment of dividends and the repayment of loans (24), and, in a bad year, trading losses (25).

If a company has a majority interest in other companies, the balance sheets and profit and loss accounts of the parent company (26) and the subsidiaries (27) are normally combined in consolidated accounts (28).

1. *bondholder* : obligataire
2. *valuation* : calcul
3. *profit* : bénéfice – benefit: avantage, allocation, prestation
4. *assets* : actifs
5. *convert* : convertir, transformer
6. *to be likely to* : avoir la chance de, être probable
7. *to earn* : gagner (a living, friends, a high interest rate)
8. *Profit & Loss Account* : compte de résultats
9. *turnover* : chiffre d'affaires
10. *overheads* : frais généraux
11. *expenditure* : dépense
12. *futher growth* : la croissance ultérieure

13. *EPS* : BPA, bénéfice par action
14. *outstanding* : en circulation, en cours
15. *cash flow statement* : tableau de financement, état des flux de trésorerie
16. *to break down* : ventiler, décomposer
17. *operating activity* : exploitation
18. *to capture* : accaparer
19. *tool* : outil
20. *bills* : factures
21. *trading profit* : bénéfice d'exploitation
22. *borrowing* : emprunt
23. *issuing of shares* : l'émission d'actions
24. *repayment of loans* : remboursement des prêts
25. *trading losses* : pertes d'exploitation
26. *parent company* : société mère
27. *subsidiaries* : filiales
28. *consolidated accounts* : comptes consolidés ou intégrés

2 Zooming on

Fundamental Analysis: The Balance Sheet

Investors often overlook the balance sheet. Assets and liabilities aren't nearly as attractive as revenue and earnings. While earnings are important, they don't tell the whole story.

The balance sheet highlights the financial condition of a company and is an integral part of the financial statements.

The balance sheet, also known as the statement of financial condition, offers a snapshot of a company's health. It tells you how much a company owns (its assets), and how much it owes (its liabilities). The difference between what it owns and what it owes is its equity, also commonly called "net assets" or "shareholders equity".

The balance sheet tells investors a lot about a company's fundamentals: how much debt the company has, how much it needs to collect from customers (and how fast it does so), how much cash and equivalents it possesses and what kinds of funds the company has generated over time.

Assets, liability and equity are the three main components of the balance sheet. Carefully analyzed, they can tell investors a lot about a company's fundamentals.

▸ Assets

There are two main types of assets: current assets and non-current assets. Current assets are likely to be used up or converted into cash within one business cycle – usually treated as twelve months. Three very important current asset items found on the balance sheet are: cash, inventories and accounts receivables.

Investors normally are attracted to companies with plenty of cash on their balance sheets. After all, cash offers protection against tough times, and it also gives companies more options for future growth. Growing cash reserves often signal strong company performance. Indeed, it shows that cash is accumulating so quickly that management doesn't have time to figure out how to make use of it. A dwindling cash pile could be a sign of trouble. That said, if loads of cash are more or less a permanent feature of the company's balance sheet, investors need to ask why the money is not being put to use. Cash could be there because management has run out of investment opportunities or is too short-sighted to know what to do with the money.

Inventories are finished products that haven't yet sold. As an investor, you want to know if a company has too much money tied up in its inventory. Companies have limited funds available to invest in inventory. To generate the cash to pay bills and return a profit, they must sell the merchandise they have purchased from suppliers. Inventory turnover (cost of goods sold) divided by average inventory) measures how quickly the company is moving merchandise through the warehouse to customers. If inventory grows faster than sales, it is almost always a sign of deteriorating fundamentals.

Receivables are outstanding (uncollected bills). Analyzing the speed at which a company collects what it's owed can tell you a lot about its financial efficiency. If a company's collection period is growing longer, it could mean problems ahead. The company may be letting customers stretch their credit in order to recognize greater top-line sales and that can spell trouble later on, especially if customers face a cash crunch. Getting money right away is preferable to waiting for it – since some of what is owed may never get paid. The quicker a company gets its customers to make payments, the sooner it has cash to pay for salaries, merchandise, equipment, loans, and best of all, dividends and growth opportunities.

Non-current assets are defined as anything not classified as a current asset. This includes items that are fixed assets, such as property, plant and equipment (PP&E). Unless the company is in financial distress and is liquidating assets, investors need not pay too much attention to fixed assets. Since companies are often unable to sell their fixed assets within any reasonable amount of time they are carried on the balance sheet at cost regardless of their actual value. As a result, it's is possible for companies to grossly inflate this number, leaving investors with questionable and hard-to-compare asset figures.

▸ Liabilities

There are current liabilities and non-current liabilities. Current liabilities are obligations the firm must pay within a year, such as payments owing to suppliers. Non-current liabilities, meanwhile, represent what the company owes in a year or more time. Typically, non-current liabilities represent bank and bondholder debt.

You usually want to see a manageable amount of debt. When debt levels are falling, that's a good sign. Generally speaking, if a company has more assets than liabilities, then it is in decent condition. By contrast, a company with a large amount of liabilities relative to assets ought to be examined with more diligence. Having too much debt relative to cash flows required to pay for interest and debt repayments is one way a company can go bankrupt

Look at the quick ratio. Subtract inventory from current assets and then divide by current liabilities. If the ratio is 1 or higher, it says that the company has enough cash and liquid assets to cover its short-term debt obligations.

$$\text{Quick Ratio} = \frac{\text{Current Assets} - \text{Inventories}}{\text{Current Liabilities}}$$

Equity

Equity represents what shareholders own, so it is often called shareholder's equity. As described above, equity is equal to total assets minus total liabilities.

Equity = Total Assets – Total Liabilities

The two important equity items are paid-in capital and retained earnings. Paid-in capital is the amount of money shareholders paid for their shares when the stock was first offered to the public. It basically represents how much money the firm received when it sold its shares. In other words, retained earnings are a tally (15) of the money the company has chosen to reinvest in the business rather than pay to shareholders. Investors should look closely at how a company puts retained capital to use and how a company generates a return on it.

Most of the information about debt can be found on the balance sheet – but some assets and debt obligations are not disclosed there. For starters, companies often possess hard-to-measure intangible assets. Corporate intellectual property (items such as patents, trademarks, copyrights and business methodologies), goodwill and brand recognition are all common assets in today's marketplace. But they are not listed on company's balance sheets.

There is also off-balance sheet debt to be aware of. This is a form of financing in which large capital expenditures are kept off of a company's balance sheet through various classification methods. Companies will often use off-balance-sheet financing to keep the debt levels low.

www.investopedia.com, by Cory Janssen

Consolidated balance sheets, IFRS

December 31	2007 EURm	2006 EURm
ASSETS		
Non-current assets		
Capitalized development costs	378	251
Goodwill	1,384	532
Other intangible assets	2,358	298
Property, plant and equipment	1,912	1,602
Investments in associated companies	325	224
Available-for-sale investments	341	288
Deferred tax assets	1,553	809
Long-term loans receivable	10	19
Other non-current assets	44	8
	8,305	4,031
Current assets		
Inventories	2,876	1,554
Accounts receivable, net of allowances for doubtful accounts (2007: EUR 332 million, 2006: EUR 212 million)	11,200	5,888
Prepaid expenses and accrued income	3,070	2,496
Current portion of long-term loans receivable	156	–
Other financial assets	239	111
Available-for-sale investments, liquid assets	4,903	5,012
Available-for-sale investments, cash equivalents	4,725	2,046
Bank and cash	2,175	1,479
	29,294	18,586
Total assets	37,599	22,617
SHAREHOLDERS'EQUITY AND LIABILITIES		
Capital and reserves attributable to equity holders of the parent		
Share capital	246	246
Share issue premium	644	2,707
Treasury shares, at cost	–3,146	–2,060
Translation differences	–163	–34
Fair value and other reserves	23	–14
Reserve for invested non-restricted equity	3,299	–
Retained earnings	13,870	11,123
	14,773	11,968
Minority interests	2,565	92
Total equity	17,338	12,060
Non-current liabilities		
Long-term interest-bearing liabilities	203	69
Deferred tax liabilities	963	205
Other long-term liabilities	119	122

	1,285	396
Current liabilities		
Current portion of long-term loans	173	–
Short-term borrowings	898	247
Accounts payable	7,074	3,732
Accrued expenses	7,114	3,796
Provisions	3,717	2,386
	18,976	10,161
Total shareholders' equity and liabilities	37,599	22,617

Useful language

actual value : valeur réelle
copyrights : droits d'auteur
dwindling : qui se réduit
to figure out : ne pas trouver
fundamentals : principes de base
to go bankrupt : faire faillite
goodwill : biens incorporels
manageable : raisonnable
to overlook : négliger
patents : brevets
questionable : contestable
quick ration : ratio de liquidité immédiate
regardless : sans se soucier
to run out of : manquer de
short-sighted : manquant de prévoyance, à courte vue
snapshot : instantané
trademarks : marques de fabrique
warehouse : entrepôt

3 Comprehension of documents

Exercice 14.1

Remplissez les blancs en utilisant les mots proposés ci-dessous.

senior accountants – bookkeepers – external auditors – management accountants – internal audit

Here are the different branches of the accounting profession presented by a British financial director.

Generally, most of the boring work – recording transactions in purchase ledgers and sales ledgers is done by.. (1) who are not qualified to a high level. The information they produce, which is basically a summary of transactions, can then be interpreted by.. (2). It can then be used by..
(3) at financial controller and director level, both for making decisions on the future of the

business, and for advising other parts of the business on how to proceed. The company's accountants also do an.. (4).

The aim of this is to ensure the management have sufficient internal control over what is going on.. (5) ensure that published financial statements give a true and fair view of the company's profit, and of its assets and liabilities.

Exercice 14.2

Remplissez les blancs en utilisant les mots proposés ci-dessous.

income less expenditure – shareholders – taxable profit – generating or consuming – income statement

He also presents different statements.

There are three or four different statements that companies include in their annual reports, which.. (1) can legally expect to see. The key documents are the profit and loss account, the balance sheet, and a funds flow statement of some kind. In the U.S., and under International Financial Reporting Standards, the profit and loss account is called an.. (2)This document is fairly self-explanatory: it is.. (3).The balance sheet is a statement showing what the company has and what it owes at the end of the year, while the funds flow statement attempts to show whether the company is.. (4) cash. The tax authorities require more detail than is given in these document; .... (5) is not the same as accounting profit, so they will expect to see reconciliations between the two.

Exercice 14.3

Trouvez pour chaque définition le mot qui lui correspond.

1. Bringing together the accounts of all a company's subsidiaries into a single set.
2. International Financial Reporting Standards.
3. Anything owned by a company – cash, buildings, machines, etc.
4. Summarising the profitability of the company by balancing revenue against expenses.
5. Calculating how much tax an individual or a company should pay – or trying to reduce this figure.
6. Checking and evaluating financial records.
7. Keeping financial records and preparing financial statements.
8. Money that a company owes to someone else – bills, debts, interest, taxes, etc.
9. Recording transactions (purchases and sales) in ledgers.
10. The use of a company's accounting data by its managers for planning and control.
11. Determining the unit cost of a manufactured product, including indirect costs.
12. The money that a company receives from supplying goods or services.
13. The money that a company spends.
14. Statement showing what the company has, and what it owes at the end of the year.

a. auditing

b. consolidation

c. management accounting

d. bookkeeping

e. liabilities

f. expenditure
g. financial accounting
h. tax accounting
i. income
j. cost accounting
k. assets
l. IFRS
m. profit and loss account
n. balance sheet

4 Practice your technical skills

Exercice 14.4

Lire les chiffres et les commenter

Lisez le document *Consolidated balance sheet, IFRS* et choisissez la proposition qui convient pour compléter les phrases.

1. Shares sell at a.. – 10p above their face value.

a. commission b. fee c. premium

1. Adjective meaning for a whole group of companies.

a. consolidated b. corporate c. merged

1. Part-ownership (less than 50%) of other companies.

a. liabilities b. conglomerate c. minority interests

1. Things of value which cannot be seen or touched, such as goodwill, brand names and trademarks.

a. expenses b. intangible assets c. tangible assets

1. The net worth of a company – the amount by which assets exceed liabilities.

a. provisions b. profit c. shareholders' equity

Exercice 14.5

Lire les chiffres et les commenter

Trouvez dans le document *Consolidated balance sheet, IFRS* les mots qui correspondent aux définitions données ci-dessous.

1. To take money that has to be repaid is to..
2. Money in notes and coins is called..
3. An amount of money lent is a..
4. .... consist of money that is expected to be received.
5. The contrary, ..., consist of money that is owed by other people.

6. Money that a company will definitely have to pay in the future, but not during the current financial year: ....

7. The entry on a balance sheet that shows how much money a business owes its suppliers for purchases made on credit: ....

8. The part of a company's profit that is retained for future reinvestment, rather than distributed as a dividend: ....

Exercice 14.6

Lire les chiffres et les commenter

Dans le document *Consolidated balance sheet, IFRS* trouvez et indiquez en lettres et en anglais les nombres correspondant aux propositions 1 à 5. Vous pouvez utiliser une calculatrice si besoin.

Nokia's consolidated balance sheets are expressed in millions of Euros; to get the total figure you need to add six zeros. For example, their provisions were €3,717,000,000: three billion, seven hundred and seventeen million Euros. These large figures can also be said as decimals: three point seven one seven billion Euros.

1. The largest figure
2. The largest negative figure
3. Total assets over the two years
4. Total equity over the two years
5. The increase in retained earnings since the previous year

FICHE 15

Méthode
Lire les chiffres et les commenter

1 STATISTIQUES

Les graphiques fournissent une image claire de la performance de l'entreprise et d'autres informations statistiques.

Exercice 15.1

Parmi les mots ci-dessous, choisissez ceux qui correspondent aux graphiques.

Exemple : 1 = *turnover remained constant*

remained constant – fluctuated – increased gradually – declined sharply – levelled off – reached a peak – fell gradually – rose sharply

1

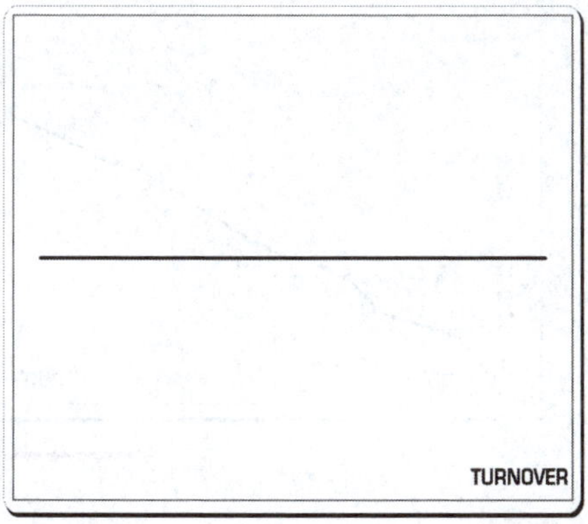

2

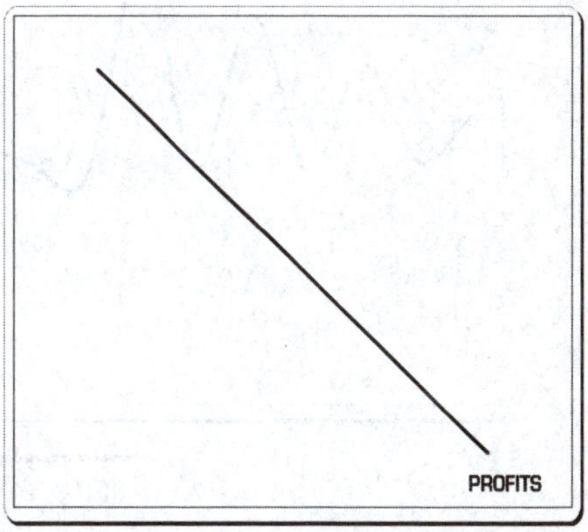

3

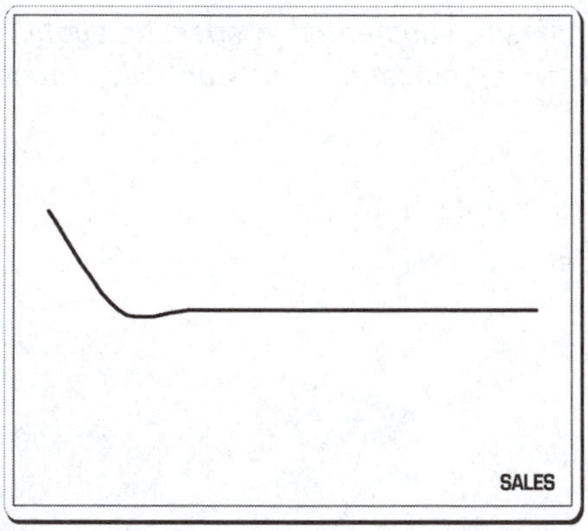

4

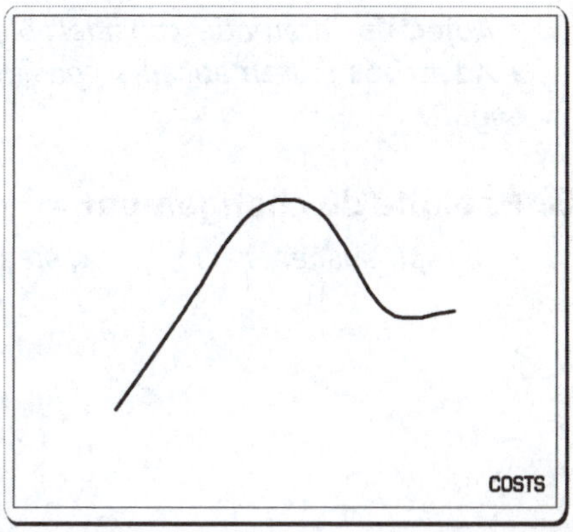

5

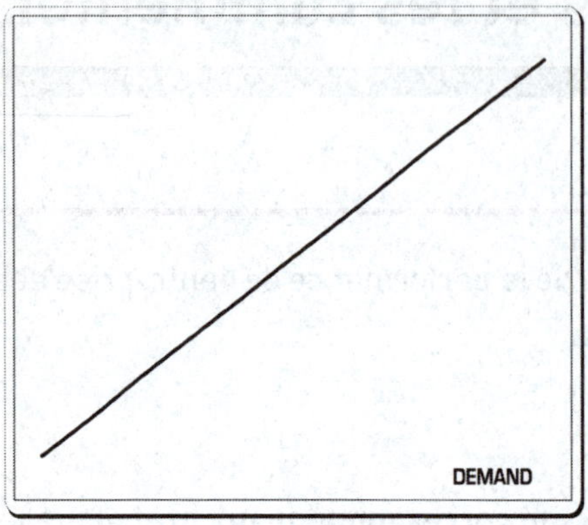

6

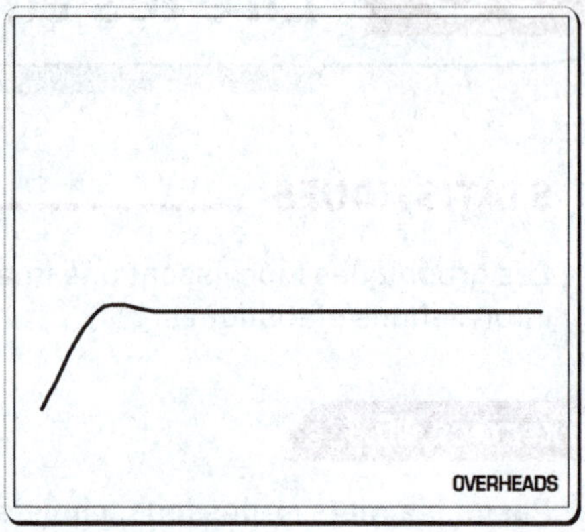

7

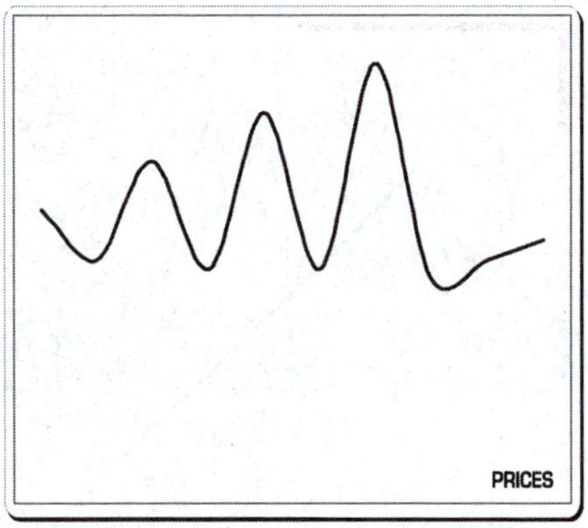

8

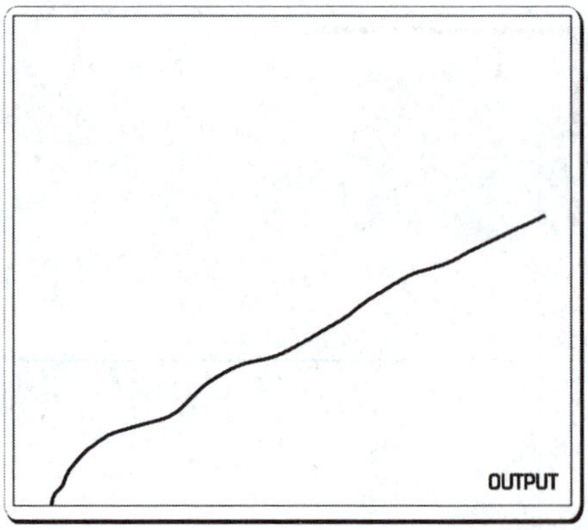

2 Parler du changement

A. Degrés du changement

- **Adjectifs** : *dramatic, considerable, sharp, significant, substantial, moderate, slight*
- **Adverbes** : *dramatically, considerably, sharply, significantly, substantially, moderately, slightly*

B. Rapidité du changement

- *Abrupt, sudden, rapid, quick, steady, gradual, slow*

C. Autres adjectifs exprimant la quantité

Adjectifs quantitatifs	Traduction
*a **hefty** salary*	un bon salaire
*banks charge customers **whopping** fees*	les banques font payer à leurs clients des frais bancaires colossaux (énormes)
***high**- interest accounts*	des comptes à taux d'intérêt élevé
*challengers have started **hiking up** rates*	les concurrents commencent à augmenter les taux
*some **huge** payouts were paid to complaining customers*	des dédommagements énormes ont été versés à des clients mécontents
***Hundreds of thousands** of people demanded compensation over the **sky-high** fees*	des centaines de milliers de gens ont exigé des compensations concernant les frais bancaires exorbitants
*the new regulations could lead to **unlimited** fines or **lengthy** prison sentences*	les nouvelles règles pourraient conduire à des amendes illimitées et à des peines de prison de longue durée
*a **wide** range of sanctions*	une gamme de sanctions étendue
*The banking market is not working properly, **largely** because most customers are not behaving as people in markets normally do*	Le marché bancaire ne fonctionne pas convenablement en grande partie parce que les clients ne se comportent pas comme les gens le font normalement dans les marchés
*a **tiny** annual interest rate*	un taux d'intérêt minuscule
*the big four offer **paltry** rates to most customers*	des taux dérisoires, (misérables)
*at a **fraction** of the cost*	pour une fraction, une petite partie du prix
*a **small** overdraft facility*	une petite autorisation de découvert
*banks make an **average** of £152 for every account held*	une moyenne de £152 sur chaque compte

D. Prépositions

*a rise **from** £ 152 to £200*
*to fall **down** to 2%* (tomber à 2%)
*to drop **by** 40%*
*to increase **by** 20%*
*an increase **of** 5.4% **over** 2 years* (une augmentation de 5,4% en 2 ans)

3 Citer des nombres

A. Prononciation du 0 en anglais

- Après les décimales
- 6.07 = *six point* oh *seven*
- Dans les années
- 1805 = *eighteen* oh *five*
- Devant la décimale
- 0.09 = *nought point* oh *nine*
- Pour le nombre
- 0 = *the number zero*

B. Le point décimal

- En anglais, on utilise un point (.) et non une virgule(,) pour les décimales. On utilise les virgules dans les nombres, les milliers par exemple (*thousands*)

• **Exemple**
20,003 : *twenty thousand and three*
20.003 : *twenty point oh oh three*

• Tous les chiffres après le point décimal se lisent séparément.

• **Exemple**
15.24 : *fifteen point two four*
0.369 : *nought point three six nine*
0.007 : *nought point oh oh seven*

• Si le nombre qui suit le point décimal est une unité d'argent, de longueur, etc., on le lit habituellement comme un nombre normal:

• **Exemple**
$30.50 : *thirty dollars fifty*
€10.99 : *ten Euros ninety nine*

C. Centaines, milliers, millions et milliards : Hundreds, thousands, millions, and billions

En anglais britannique, on utilise ***and*** après ***hundred*** ; pas en anglais américain.

2, 345, 678, 120	
British English	**American English**
two billion, three hundred and forty-five million, six hundred and seventy-eight thousand, one hundred and twenty	two billion, three hundred forty-five million, six hundred seventy-eight thousand, one hundred twenty

D. Fractions

Les fractions sont presque comme les chiffres ordinaux (fifth, sixth, thirty first, forty third, etc.) :
a half : ½
a third : 1/3
a quarter : ¼
three quarters : ¾
a fifth : 1/5
a sixth : 1/6
three and a half : 3 ½
two and three quarters : 2 ¾

FICHE 16

La stratégie de l'entreprise

1 Ground work

Corporate Strategy

The direction an organization takes with the objective of achieving and sustaining business success in the long term. A number of models have been used to develop corporate strategy. Yet, it rarely rises to that level, despite an abundance of corporate strategy theory and significant research from many organisations over the past few decades.

More recent approaches have focused on the need for companies:

- to adapt to and anticipate changes in the business environment.
- to establish the purpose and scope (1) of the organization's activities in a creative manner
- to examine the nature of the business it is in
- to take into consideration the environment in which it operates, its position in the marketplace, and the competition it faces
- to align (2) policies, practices, and resources to realise that vision

Most managers believe that a corporate strategy implies a strong focus on **competition**, since competition takes place almost exclusively at the offering level. Most organisations concentrate their strategic efforts on constantly improving (3) **the goods and services** they offer. This overemphasis (4) on the temporary success, however, can often obscure the kind of thinking and emphasis that would lead to sustained success, even a continuous repetition of temporary successes doesn't equate to (5) sustainable strategy. In an effort to increase the value of single offerings, the organisation may be distracted (6) from larger questions of structure, mission and objective.

Although corporate strategy can be very goal-oriented (7), especially in the early stages of a company's development, the very nature of goals implies temporary success. By contrast, sustainable success is not, and cannot be an end unto itself or a goal to achieve. Therefore, goal orientation becomes arguably inappropriate when success has to be indefinitely sustained.

Despite this, an overwhelming number of top executives and researchers make extensive use of objectives in their **quest of lasting corporate success**. Certainly, a number of factors contribute to this: the need of leaders with limited tenure (8) to point to achievements (9), the tyranny of **meeting the expectations of the financial markets** and most management teams extensively rely on (10) forecasting (11) and planning. Still, the idea held by most managers that strategy itself is all about goal achievement only exacerbates the situation. Therefore, it is important for strategists to remember that the more specific an objective, the further away it may potentially lead the organisation from its optimal big picture.

So how strategy should be redefined? Clearly it cannot rely too strongly on objectives nor can it focus too heavily on **competition**. A more fundamental concept is needed to guide an organisation in seeing its big picture, and such concept should be customer. To create sustainable, long-term success, an organisation must first and fundamentally understand and relate to (12) its **customers**. It is the ongoing encouragement of this understanding, based on neither specific competitors nor temporal objectives, which must be at the heart of any real strategy. And it is that from which all objectives should naturally flow.

C.K Prahalad, a specialist in corporate strategy, believed firms should seek not simply to position themselves well within their existing markets but **to capitalise on their advantages** to redefine markets in their favour. That, he argued, involves identifying and developing strengths (13) that cannot easily be imitated by competitors. Firms should then stretch those skills (14) to the maximum, setting themselves ambitious and industry-transforming goals, and using those goals to galvanise (15) their workers.

He was particularly struck by the ability of Japanese firms to harness (16) the ideas of their humbler employees.

Later in his career, he became increasingly fascinated by **innovation**. He argued that company-centric (17) innovation was giving way to "co-creation" (18), in which firms collaborate with their customers and business allies.

He also shifted his attention to companies waking up to the fact that technological innovation and economic reform were opening up new markets in poorer countries and growing in confidence (19). He taught the world's biggest companies to think of themselves anew, as a "portfolio (20) of competencies" rather than as a "portfolio of businesses". He taught everyone to see the developing world as a vortex (21) of innovation and creativity.

New processes, that thoroughly change the way innovative low cost products are made and delivered, have been dubbed "disruptive (22) innovation".

Most Western managers deal with problems of management with repeated cost-cutting (23). But the experience of the emerging markets indicates that **"cost innovation"** —rebuilding an entirely new design for both products and processes- without making use of what has been done before— to reduce costs is a much cheaper and simpler strategy.

There is obviously **a trend away from premium-priced design features** and toward simpler, more basic designs. Understanding this challenging shift in consumer behaviour is necessary for companies to compete successfully. It represents an opportunity for those that respond quickly and effectively to differentiate themselves from their peers.

1. *scope* : étendue, portée, limites
2. *to align* : aligner, cadrer [«'lain]
3. *improve* : améliorer
4. *overemphasis* : accentuation excessive
5. *to equate to* : mettre sur le même pied, être assimilable à
6. *distracted* : distrait
7. *goal-oriented* : axé sur les objectifs
8. *little tenure* : occupation de poste de courte durée
9. *to point to achievements* : montrer les réalisations
10. *to rely on* : s'appuyer sur, compter sur
11. *forecasting* : prévision
12. *to relate to* : établir un lien
13. *strength* : force, point fort
14. *skills* : compétences
15. *to galvanise* : pousser à agir
16. *to harness* : atteler
17. *company-centric innovation* : innovation axée sur l'entreprise
18. *co-création* : création en co-opération

19. *confidence* : confiance
20. *portfolio* : portefeuille
21. *vortex* : tourbillon
22. *disruptive* : perturbatrice
23. *cost-cutting* : réduction de coût

2 Zooming on

Northern Foods PLC

Established in 1937, we supply great tasting food to all the major supermarkets, including Ready Meals, Sandwiches and Salads, Pizza, Biscuits and Puddings across the three areas of Chilled, Frozen and Bakery production. In each of its core markets, Northern Foods has strong leading brands or high growth, own label positions.

We are building a strong platform for growth around our core categories.

Northern Foods is committed to generating the best possible returns for its shareholders. We are driving a comprehensive change programme to create a more focused and competitive company, capable of driving improved shareholder returns.

Financial information

This section provides the latest financial information from Northern Foods as reported at the 2007/08 half year results on 13 November 2007.

Operating highlights

- Continued progress against all elements of the performance improvement plan.
- Chilled improvement continues, with underlying revenue up 5.4% and operating margin up by 200 basis points.
- Repositioning of Fox's progressing on plan.
- Launch of Goodfella's into the chilled category with "Goodfella's Signatore".
- Recovery of recent commodity cost increases agreed.

Northern-Foods.co.UK

Financial highlights

Unaudited 26 weeks	To 29 Sept 2007	To 30 Sept 2006	Increase/ (decrease)
Continuing operations			
Revenue	**£438.6m**	£427.8m	2.5%
Profit from operations	**£26.8m**	£25.3m	5.9%
Operating margin	**6.1%**	5.9%	3.4%
Profit before tax	**£20.1m**	£14.6m	37.7%
Adjusted eps	**3.21p**	2.39p	34.3%
As reported – statutory			
Profit for the period (after tax)	**£15.0m**	£30.5m	(50.8%)
Dividend per share	**1.55p**	1.50p	3.3%

Chilled

Revenue up 5.4% to £229.4m (2006/07: £217.7m)

Profit from operations up 61.9% to £13.6m (2006/07: £8.4m)

Frozen
Revenue down 2.8% to £117.8m (2006/07: £121.2m)
Profit from operations down 37.8% to £6.1m (2006/07: £9.8m)
Bakery
Revenue increased by 2.8% to £91.4m (2006/07: £88.9m)
Profit from operations maintained on prior year at £7.1m (2006/07: £7.1m)
Northern-foods.co.UK

Group strategy

Northern Foods is a focused company that has chosen to operate in five markets and seeks to drive improved shareholder returns by:

- focusing on growth markets;
- working with customers that value quality and service;
- operating a low-cost business model.

Today's Northern Foods is the result of significant change, resulting from the implementation of our comprehensive performance improvement plan. In order to create this more competitive and resilient business, the following actions were initiated:

• The disposal of businesses accounting for around 40% of group revenue – with proceeds being used to reduce borrowings, reduce the pension deficit and invest for growth. The sale process was completed in January 2007.

• Simplification of the Chilled business in order to improve returns, reduce costs and enhance our ability to serve our customers.

• A clear focus on central cost reductions to reflect the simpler, focused Northern Foods.

• Rigorous capital and cash management in order to drive improved shareholder value.

As part of its shaping the Future Business Review announced on May 31 2006, Northern Foods indicated that it proposed disposing of businesses representing approximately 40 per cent of group revenue in order to focus on fewer, higher performing categories.

The disposals, which were completed on 13 January 2007, will support reduced complexity in the business, improve focus and thus drive improved performance, earnings and cash flow, creating a more competitive, resilient business. In total, gross proceeds of £211.2 million were received from the disposal programme and the overall process was completed in under eight months, ahead of the full calendar year target.

The businesses in the disposal programme comprised:

- Smiths Flour Milling and NFT Distribution, which were non-core businesses;
- Cakes and Speciality Bread, which Northern Foods anticipated would continue to trade with lower margins, relative to their chosen categories;
- Chilled Pastry Products, which had significant upside potential but required major investment.

Northern-foods.co.UK

Northern Foods Passes on Rising Costs to Customers

Northern Foods, the maker of Goodfella's pizza and Fox's biscuits, yesterday cheered the market with results at the top end of expectations, assuring investors it was coping with rising costs of ingredients by passing them on to customers.

The company conceded its frozen foods arm had a disappointing year partly because a cold, wet summer hit the barbecue season, but said that its chilled and bakery businesses grew strongly, helped by a new Christmas pudding launch Despite higher prices for cereals, dairy products, cocoa and fats, the supplier of ready-meals, salads and sandwiches to big supermarkets managed to improve its margins. It reported pre-tax profits

from continuing operations up more than 25% to £50.1m in the year to March 29, compared with £40m a year earlier.
Overall, ingredients costs were almost 5% higher than the year before but Northern Foods said it passed on some of that burden in higher prices for its products. It plans to impose more price rises.
Chief executive Stefan Barden flagged up progress with the company's strategy to come up with product lines that shoppers buy repeatedly while getting out of low-margin, underperforming businesses. Although the company raised its full-year dividend 5.9% to 4.5p per share, Barden remained cautious about the year ahead.
"The current trading environment remains challenging, with continuing commodity cost pressures which we are committed to recovering", he said. "Despite some caution, we expect the underlying business to continue to make good progress in 2008-09 (abriged).

Cartoon by Englehart *Caglecartoons.com*

The Guardian, May 28th, 2008,
by Katie Allen

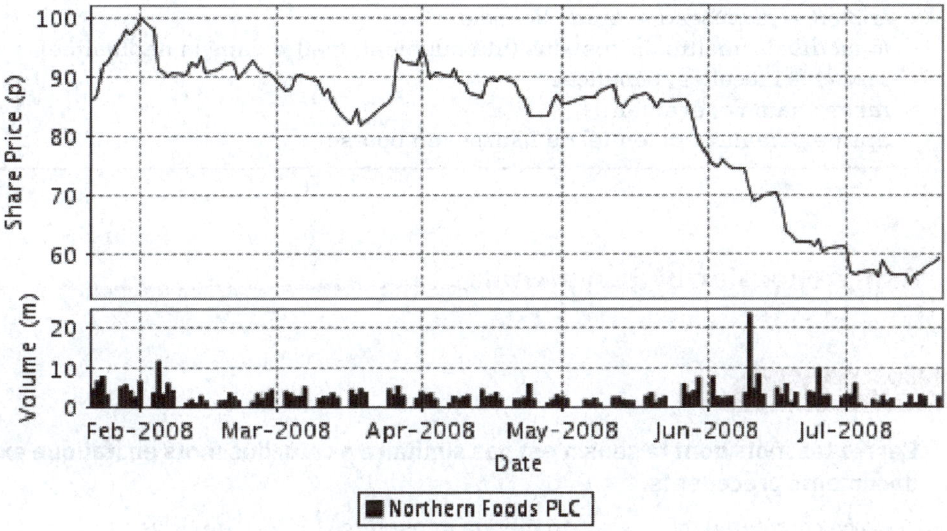

Northern Foods PLC is listed on the London Stock Exchange and is a constituent of the FTSE 250 Index

Jobs at Risk as Supermarket Supplier Abandons M&S Contract

More than 700 workers could lose their jobs after Northern Foods abandoned its contract to make Italian ready-meals for Marks & Spencer, saying that it could not make a profit on the deal (1).
Northern Foods is to mothball (2) its Fenland Foods factory in Grantham, which produces a range (3) of chilled Italian meals for M&S.
After long-running contract discussions with M&S, Northern Foods said it was unable to reach an agreement under which it could make a profit. It now hopes to land a deal with another supermarket chain…

Stefan Barden, chief executive, said: "We have to be prepared to have the site closed for two to three years. Quite frankly, you can't keep people employed through that time period."
A spokeswoman said: "The factory is not designed (4) in a productive and efficient way. It is 20 years old and a complicated site."
She insisted the factory could reopen, after substantial investment, in two years time.
Staff who are laid off (5) are to get preferential treatment if they apply for a job at Fenland in the future. Some staff will be offered alternative roles at other sites.
The rising cost of food has also put suppliers under pressure, as supermarkets are reluctant to pass increases on to shoppers. Shares in Northern Foods fell 3p to 85.5p.

The Guardian, May 14th, 2008,
by Graeme Weardon and Julia Finch

Useful language

to cheer : réconforter, remonter le moral
completed : achevé
deal : transaction, affaire
designed : conçu
to enhance : accroître, améliorer
to flag up : marquer, signaler
implementation : exécution, mise en œuvre
laid off = *dismissed* = *fired* : licencié
to mothball : mettre en suspens (littéralement, mettre dans la naphtaline)
proceeds : recettes, bénéfices
range : gamme, éventail
upside potential : potentiel de hausse (en bourse)

3 Comprehension of documents

Exercice 16.1

Barrez les mots dont le sens n'est pas similaire à celui des mots en italique extraits des documents précédents.

1. *to be committed to*	to pledge oneself to	to drive
2. *to cope with*	to deal with	to adapt to
3. *comprehensive*	complete	expanding
4. *proceeds*	increments	earnings
5. *to reduce*	to cut	to eliminate
6. *a deal*	a transaction	a merger

Exercice 16.2

Reliez chaque verbe à un groupe nominal pour former une expression correcte.

1. to launch
2. to be committed to
3. to mothball
4. to reach
5. to recover
6 to dispose of
7. to cope with
8. to reinforce
9. to make
10. to apply for
11. to account for

a. good progress
b. a product's reputation
c. cost increases
d. 40% of group revenue
e. generating returns
f. a new type of pizza
g. an agreement
h. rising costs
i. a factory
j. non-core businesses
k. a job

4 Practice your technical skills

Exercice 16.3

Lire les chiffres et les commenter

Le texte présente une analyse du graphique *Northern Foods in 2008*. Complétez les blancs en utilisant la forme correcte des verbes proposés (a-i).

a. go down
b. plummet
c. rally
d. firm
e. decline
f. flutuate
g. fall
h. drop
i. peak

Shares in Northern Foods started the year at around 87p, and.. at 100p in February, following the announcement that they had completed the sale of non-core businesses. In early spring they.. back to 90p and then.. over the next two months when they.. even further to 81p, affected by the spiralling prices of ingredients – almost 5% higher than the year before. In April shares.. to 93p before fluctuating again till the end of May when they.. to 76p. In June the shares gradually.. to 60p and they.. to a new low of 55p in July and then.. slightly to 60p at the end of the month.

Exercice 16.4

La note de synthèse

Rédigez une note de synthèse en anglais (235 à 265 mots) sur les changements important de Northern Foods, en faisant ressortir les objectifs de l'entreprise et leurs conséquences économiques.

FICHE 17

Les chocs pétroliers et leurs conséquences

1 Ground work

Oil Crises

▸ **The issues (1)**

• Fossil fuels are a finite (2) resource : coal, natural gas, and petrol can be extracted from the earth only as long as they last.
• Price variation is enormous due to:
– market forces of supply and demand
– speculation
– geopolitical factors
• The world has been shaken (3) time and again by sudden very high price increases : these oil shocks happened in 1973, 1979 and, more recently, in 2008. They caused economic recession, inflation and unemployment (4).

▸ **How supply and demand influence oil prices**

O.P.E.C., the organisation of petrol exporting countries : Iran, Iraq, Kuwait, Saudi Arabia, Venezuela, Qatar, Indonesia, Libya, the Unites Arab Emirates, Algeria, Nigeria, Ecuador and Angola, tries to coordinate oil production in order to stabilise prices.

Emerging (5) industrial powers require more and more energy: the growing motor car production in India and China will increase the need for fuel, while supplies cannot increase. Scarcity (6) and shortages (7) cause price rises.

Speculation means that oil is traded as a commodity (8) on international stock markets (9) and the price is pushed up in futures markets (10).

▸ **The geopolitical factors triggering oil shocks**

1973: During the Yom Kippur war opposing Israel against Egypt and Syria, the USA suffered an oil embargo because they supported Israel. OPEC reduced oil production in order to raise prices.
1979: Oil production was disrupted (11) in Iran and Iraq because of the revolution and the Iran-Iraq war.

▸ **Other crises and price rises**

1990: Prices rose following the Gulf war
2000: Record high price due to OPEC production cuts.
2004: Shortages were the aftermath (12) of the invasion of Iraq
2008: The highest-ever price for oil (close to 150 dollars a barrel) was reached, but this seemed more due to speculation than other factors.
(There were also some price slumps (13), as in 1986 due to overproduction and in 2009 after the world financial crisis)
2010: As we go to print (14) , it seems that prices are reaching record highs again.

▸ **Are there alternative solutions?**

1. There is a need for energy saving (15) measures to reduce demand. Using public transport and cycling (16) are being encouraged in European towns. Proper (17) home insulation (18) to prevent heat loss (19) can be promoted.

2. Alternative energy supplies were sought while demand remained high. France has developed nuclear power (20) . Meanwhile, other renewable (21) sources of energy have been developed like wind farms (22) and solar panels (23).
A biofuel, Ethanol, is produced from corn, and can be used for motor-car engines.

None of these solutions is perfect: there is the problem of nuclear waste; wind farms spoil the landscape and it has been argued that more energy is used to create biofuel than it saves.

What is certain is that petrol is running out (24). The world will have to learn to do without it (25).

1. *the issue* : le sujet du débat
2. *finite* : limité
3. *shaken* : secoué
4. *unemployment* : chômage
5. *emerging* : en voie de développement
6. *scarcity* : pénurie
7. *shortages* : manques
8. *commodity* : matière première
9. *stock market* : bourse
10. *futures market* : marché à terme
11. *disrupted* : perturbé
12. *aftermath* : consequence, après-coup
13. *slump* : forte baisse
14. *to go to print* : être prêt à imprimer
15. *energy saving* : économie d'énergie
16. *cycling* : aller à vélo
17. *proper* : efficace, comme il faut
18. *insulation* : isolation thermique
19. *heat loss* : perte de chaleur
20. *nuclear power* : énergie nucléaire
21. *renewable* : renouvelable
22. *wind farms* : parcs d'éoliennes
23. *solar panels* : panneaux solairez
24. *to run out* : (une reserve) s'épuiser rapidement
25. *to do without* : se passer de

2 Zooming on

Ryanair warns high oil prices could slash its profits by 50% next year

Budget airline Ryanair warned today that profits could fall by up to 50% next year on the back of high oil prices, declining consumer spending and the weakening pound.
Chief executive Michael O'Leary said the European airline sector faces the possibility of a "perfect storm" of higher oil prices, poor consumer demand, weaker sterling and higher costs and there is now "a significant chance" that profits in 2008/09 will decline.
"At our most optimistic, a combination of flat yields and $75 oil would see profits grow by 6% to approximately €500m, but at our most conservative, if forward oil prices remain at $85, and consumer sentiment/sterling weakness leads to a 5% reduction in yields, then profits in the coming year could fall by as much as 50% to as low as £175m (€235m)," he said.
Shares in Ryanair tumbled more than 10% on the stark profits warning, falling to €3.21.

Rival budget airlines were also hit, with easyJet down by 6%.

But the Ryanair boss later told journalists at a press conference in London that he would welcome a recession, as it would allow the airline to keep its prices low and would also depress fuel costs across the industry.

Asked if he was concerned about the chill that appears to be spreading across the sector, he said: "Not a lot. In many ways we would welcome a chill or something even colder.

"We would welcome a good, deep, bloody recession for 12 to 18 months.

"One, it would lead to lower fares and, two, it would expose the regulatory scam that is going on over here," a reference to the group's long-running argument with the Civil Aviation Authority over airport charges.

O'Leary also claimed that a recession would put an end to the "environmental bullshit among the chattering classes that has allowed Gordon Brown to double air passenger duty. We need a recession if we are going to see off some of this environmental nonsense."

He dismissed fears that an economic downturn would lead to lower passenger numbers for the group, saying he expects growth to continue at double- digit rates. But profits will be hit as the airline slashes prices to maintain demand.

O'Leary's warning on profits came as the group, Europe's largest low-cost airline, reported a worse-than-expected 27% fall in third-quarter profits, to €35m (£25.54m).

The Ryanair boss described it as "creditable performance in very adverse market conditions", and said he still expects profits for the current year to be ahead by around 17.5% to €470m.

guardian.co.uk, February 4th, 2008,
by Fiona Walsh and Dan Milmo

Useful language

bullshit : (grossier) conneries
chattering classes (the) : les intellectuels qui s'écoutent parler
chill : refroidissement, coup de froid
dismiss fears : balayer les craintes
double-digit : à deux chiffres
downturn : baisse, ralentissement
duty : taxe
profit warning : annonce d'une baisse prochaine des bénéfices d'une entreprise
scam : arnaque, escroquerie
see off : dire au revoir, chasser
slash prices : cut, reduce, decrease

3 Comprehension of document

Exercice 17.1

Choisissez la proposition qui convient pour compléter les phrases.

1. Ryanair faces serious challenges and could see

a. economic turbulence put a brake on profits.

b. its fuel bill decrease.

c. higher passenger demand.

2. Ryanair's future profits are likely to

a. rally.

b. be halved.

c. triple.

3. Budget carriers struggle to defy the crisis :

a. other low-cost airlines reported a small profit.

b. easyjet was not hit.

c. Ryanair disappointed investors.

4. According to Michael O'Leary a recession would result in

a. a depressed fuel bill across the industry;

b. slashed ticket prices.

c. both a. and b.

5. Which of the following does not apply when a recession bites?

a. new jobs and a more creative period

b. a plunge in the shares of budget airlines

c. growth over 9%

6. Ryanair' s boss also blamed .... for the current slump

a. unjustifiably rising airport taxes

b. the lack of environmental concern

c. fleet expansion

7. Michael O'Leary raised fears of

a. a severe slowdown in 2009.

b. lean years for shareholders.

c. more expensive fares.

8. With the worsening economic outlook, the company's third-quarter results

a. came as no surprise at all.

b. were considered acceptable.

c. began to spiral.

Exercice 17.2

Reformulez les phrases en complétant les blancs.

1. Budget airline Ryanair warned today that profits could fall by up to 50% next year on the back of high oil prices.

The higher……………………………………the lower……………………………………

2. Profits could fall by up to 50 per cent.

Profits…………………………………… be likely to……………………………………

3. We would welcome a good, deep, bloody recession for 12 to 18 months.

We would welcome a…………………………………… recession.

4. We need a recession if we are going to see off some of this environmental nonsense.

We are not going to see off some of this environmental nonsense…………………………………… (*sauf si*) our economy moves into recession.

5. But profits will be hit as the airline slashes prices to maintain demand.

When the airline…………………………………… prices to maintain demand, profits ……………………………………

4 Practice your technical skills

Exercice 17.3

La traduction

Traduisez.

1. Higher fuel costs are partly offset (compenser) by dollar weakness.
2. Budget carriers' shares look more and more vulnerable.
3. Low-cost air fares are bumped up by extras. Ryanair is the worst culprit (coupable).
4. The chief executive expressed hope that a downturn would weed out (comme se débarrasser des mauvaises herbes) weaker rivals.
5. Low-cost fares are not as competitive as they used to be.
6. Ryanair's ultra-frugal approach to flying means the lowest fares and the best punctuality.

"[…] saying he expects growth to continue at double-digit rates"
Notez que les deux parties du mot composé sont séparées par un trait d'union et que le nom lui-même digit ne prend jamais la forme du pluriel car précédent le nom rates il le qualifie et devient invariable comme un adjectif.

• **Exemple**
a ten-minute break, a three-mile walk, fifty-penny stamps.

Exercice 17.4

La traduction

Traduisez.

1. un contrat de quinze pages
2. un billet de cent dollars
3. un discours de trois heures

Exercice 17.5

La correspondance

Lisez la lettre envoyée à John Fields dans laquelle Ferial Galal signale des erreurs et refuse de payer le prix convenu. Choisissez les expressions appropriées pour chaque numéro.

Ferial Galal, Marketing Director of World Golfing Ltd, placed an order for an advertisement with an agency. On 31 March she stated the following requirements to John Fields at London Media :

- Publication : Hype magazine
- Last date for submission of text : 1 May
- Issue date : 18 May
- Position : as specified – no alternative position accepted
- Payment : on last day of month following publication
- Advertisement to be approved before publication

It is now 28 June. Ferial Galal has just received a copy of the latest issue of Hype magazine with the advertisement in it. She has noticed that the advertisement did not appear as requested.

WORLD GOLFING Ltd

34 Old Street
London
EC 1V 9HQ

John Fields
London Media
113 Kensington High Street
28 June

Dear John

I have **1** (just received / just got) the latest issue of your magazine and checked our advertisement. I'm **2** (unhappy / sorry) to tell you that a number of mistakes have been made by London Media. I wrote to you on 31 March **3** (confirming / saying) the details of the advertisement. **4** (Unfortunately / And) the following mistakes have **5** (come up / occurred):

- The advertisement appeared in the issue of 27 June instead of 1 May.
- It was on a right-hand page instead of a left-hand page.
- It was placed in the last part of the magazine. We **6** (instructed / specified) that it should be in the front part.

We **7** (insisted / made it clear) that the correct position of the advertisement was **8** (absolutely vital / the most important thing). As you can imagine, the incorrect placing of the advertisement has caused us great **9** (distress / inconvenience) and will no doubt **10** (affect / boost) sales of our new product range. Due to all these errors, we **11** (don't want to / feel unable to) pay the full cost of the advertisement. I am, however, prepared to pay 30 per cent of the cost and trust that you **12** (like the idea / consider this acceptable).

I look forward to **13** (receiving / hearing) your comments **14** (as soon as possible / quickly).

Yours sincerely

Ferial Galal
Ferial Galal
Marketing Director

Exercice 17.6

La correspondance

Mettez les phrases dans l'ordre pour retrouver l'organisation habituelle d'une lettre de réclamation.

1. Explain what went wrong or why you were dissatisfied.
2. Mention the inconvenience caused.
3. End with appropriate comment.
4. Begin by regretting the need to complain.
5. Suggest how the matter can be put right or what your solution to the problem is.

Relisez la lettre de Ferial Galal et observez la façon dont elle organise ses idées.

Exercice 17.7

La correspondance

Rédigez votre propre lettre de réclamation, en vous appuyant sur l'énoncé suivant.

Vous avez passé commande de 200 compact discs le 15 mars et quand ils vous ont été livrés, vous en avez trouvé 20 gravement rayés.

L'emballage qui les contenait semblait en parfait état et vous avez accepté la livraison et signé sans faire d'objection (without question). C'est à l'ouverture du paquet que les dégâts ont été découverts. Vous ne faites que supposer que cela est dû à de mauvaises manipulations (careless handling) avant l'emballage.

Vous joignez une liste des articles endommagés et vous apprécieriez qu'ils soient remplacés. Vous les avez conservés au cas où votre expéditeur en aurait besoin pour réclamer une compensation à ses fournisseurs.

Formule de politesse.

FICHE 18

Les traits contemporains des échanges internationaux

1 Ground work

International Trade

▶ **What is it?**

Trade is an exchange of goods and services. International trade between countries involves (1) imports (2) and exports (3) of goods (4) which are produced in different places. Some countries need to import what they lack (5) from others that produce more. These goods can be raw materials (6), food, manufactured goods (7), or invisible services like insurance (8).

Free trade (9) would mean that there would be no barriers (10) such as customs duty (11) to stop the movement of goods; protectionism, on the other hand, could be used by states to defend the interests of their own producers by preventing (12) cheap imports.

▶ **Organisations ruling international trade.**

The **GATT** (General Agreement on Tariffs and Trade) was set up (13) in 1947 as rounds (14) of negotiations between trading nations to reach agreements (15) on reducing barriers to trade.

The Uruguay round created the W.T.O. (World Trade Organisation) (16) in 1995. The W.T.O. has its headquarters (17) in Geneva.
153 countries make up (18) the membership of the WTO of which 117 are developing countries.
Russia, however, is not a member.
The head is Pascal Lamy, a Frenchman.
It aims (19) to "help producers of goods and services, exporters and importers, conduct (20) their business". The free flow (21) of trade is supposed to increase member countries' wealth (22).

▶ **How the WTO works**

It sets up (13) trade negotiations: the latest round started in Doha in 2001.
It checks (23) that trading rules are respected
It settles (24) trade disputes: there are a great number of these. Examples of disputes between the US and the EU were about preferential tariffs for importation of Carribean (25) bananas and about the ban on hormone-containing meat imports from America.

▶ **Pros and Cons**

The reduction of barriers for agricultural produce, such as are imposed by the US and the EU, would encourage exports from developing countries (The WTO aims to help them).

Nothing is done, however, within the WTO framework (26), to ensure that workers rights are protected. The anti-free-trade (27) movement points out that world-wide (28) results are harmful (29) in effects on poverty and ecology.

1. *involver* : concerne
2. *imports* : importations
3. *exports* : exportations
4. *goods* : les biens, les marchandises
5. *to lack* : manquer de
6. *raw materials* : matières premières
7. *manufactured goods* : produits manufacturés
8. *insurance* : assurance
9. *free trade* : libre échange
10. *barriers* : obstacles
11. *customs duty* : droits de douane
12. *to prevent* : empêcher de
13. *to set up* : mettre en place
14. *a round* : une série récurrente
15. *to reach agreements* : arriver à des accords
16. *World Trade Organisation* : Organisation mondiale du Commerce
17. *headquarters* : quartier général
18. *make up* : composent
19. *to aim to* : avoir pour objectif de
20. *to conduct* : mener
21. *free flow* : libre circulation
22. *wealth* : richesse
23. *to check* : verifier
24. *to settle* : apaiser, résoudre
25. *Carribean* : Antillais
26. *framework* : le cadre d'une organisation
27. *anti-free-trade* : altermondialiste
28. *world-wide* : mondial
29. *harmful* : nocif

2 Zooming on

Fair enough?

Cadbury hopes to secure its cocoa supply with a new scheme.

Times have not been sweet lately for Cadbury Schweppes, the world's biggest confectioner by sales. Nelson Peltz, an American activist investor, is waging a campaign for more influence over the management of the British company. Prices for raw materials are at record highs. Policymakers are stepping up their campaigns to warn consumers about the dangers of obesity. And Cadbury is uncertain about how to proceed with its plan to demerge its fizzy-drinks business, given the turbulence in the financial markets.

So the company's announcement of its "Cadbury Cocoa Partnership" on January 28th provided a helpful distraction from such problems. Cadbury will spend £44m ($87m) over ten years to finance the partnership, starting with a £1m investment in a seed fund this year, and increasing to £5m a year from 2010. The aim of the venture is to show cocoa farmers how to increase yields using fertilisers and by working with each other. It will also help them to find additional sources of income by encouraging them to plant red peppers and mangoes, which can grow beneath cocoa trees, and coconuts, which can grow above them. Moreover, Cadbury has commissioned 850 water wells, serving 150 to 200 people each, which will give women and children liberated from water-fetching duties time to do other things. It intends to finance schools, teachers and libraries.

Is there another motive for the ostensibly philanthropic venture? Without cocoa supplies from Ghana, Cadbury would be in big trouble. The west African country provides all of the cocoa for Cadbury's British operations and 70% of its worldwide supply. Cadbury says Ghanaian high-quality cocoa gives Dairy Milk, Creme Egg and other Cadbury treats their distinctive taste. It buys one-tenth of the crop produced in Ghana, which is the second-biggest producer after Côte-d'Ivoire.

Alarm bells started to ring at the firm's headquarters when a Cadbury-financed study by the University of Sussex and the University of Accra found that the average production of a cocoa farmer had dropped to 40% of potential yield, and that the children of cocoa farmers did not want to work in the family business any more. Ghanaian farmers have six children on average and farm tiny plots of land of around two hectares. Some have annual incomes of as little as £450.

So Cadbury decided to do something that it hopes will secure its supply – and make it look virtuous. It could have signed up to Fairtrade, an international social movement that promotes the payment of above-market prices to producers of agricultural commodities in developing countries by setting a floor price, with an additional premium that goes to farmers for reinvestment and social projects. "But we found that productivity, not price, was the problem," says Alex Cole of Cadbury. Ghanaian cocoa trades at 10% above the average world price of £1,176 per tonne. So Cadbury devised a scheme of its own that is similar to Fairtrade in some respects, but gives it greater flexibility over the terms. (Cadbury does use Fairtrade cocoa from Belize for Green & Black's "Maya Gold", a niche chocolate brand.)

Other firms have done similar things. Starbucks has a scheme called CAFE through which the coffee-house chain encourages farmers to improve quality and supports social projects. (It also buys some coffee on Fairtrade terms.) Mars, the biggest American chocolate-maker, does not sell any Fairtrade products in spite of loud clamouring from campaigners, but last year pledged $4.5m over three years for a scheme to improve cocoa farming in west Africa, run in partnership with four non-governmental organisations and a development agency.

This week Fairtrade campaigners gave Cadbury's scheme a guarded welcome. "We welcome Cadbury's initiative to support Ghanaian cocoa farmers and their communities, and we will be looking to the company to ensure that principles of sustainable production and fair trade are embedded at the heart of their initiative," says Barbara Crowther of the Fairtrade Foundation in London.

Fairtrade and large corporations do not sit naturally together. Fairtrade's price-adjustment mechanism is intended to insulate small producers from volatile commodity markets and the free-trading, no-holds-barred capitalism that multinational companies espouse. But firms are finding ways to improve the lot of small farmers, and burnish their own reputations, without signing up to Fairtrade's rules. Are such "Fairtrade lite" strategies a rejection of Fairtrade's approach – or are they a backhanded compliment?

January 31st, 2008,
The Economist print edition

The big issue

Degree of priority given to corporate responsibility, %

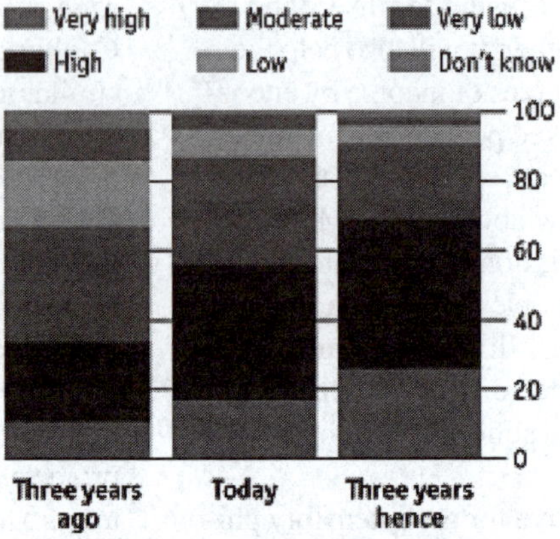

Source: Economist Intelligence Unit, Global Business Barometer, an online survey of 1,192 global executives, Nov-Dec 2007

Useful language

average : moyen
clamouring : un tollé
confectioner : confiseur
to demerge : scinder
embedded : imbriqué, gravé dans
to farm : cultiver
floor price : prix seuil
lite : used to describe foods or drinks that contain few calories or low amounts of sugar, fat or alcohol. Ex: lite beer, lite yoghurt.
NGO : ONG
no-holds-barred : aucune prise interdite (sport)
peppers : piments
philanthropic venture : entreprise périlleuse
pledge : promesse, engagement
seed : graine
the terms : les conditions
water wells : puits

3 Comprehension of documents

Exercice 18.1

Répondez en anglais aux questions suivantes.

1. Explain the pun in the title.
2. Describe the various difficulties encountered by Cadbury Schweppes.
3. What issue expressed in the headline does the document deal with?

4. What commitment did Cadbury Schweppes make to West Africa?
5. What motivates companies to get involved in fair trade? Might there be room for cynicism?
6. What is really alarming in Ghana?
7. How does Cadbury Schweppes' action compare with Fairtrade's?
8. Quote two companies that use original schemes to protect their reputation.
9. How did Fairtrade react to Cadbury Schweppes' new strategy?
10. What shortcoming(s) of corporate social responsibility is/are highlighted in the last paragraph?

Exercice 18.2

Répondez aux questions suivantes.

1. Is the last sentence of paragraph 1 a cause or a consequence of the sentence before?
2. "the company's announcement of its "Cadbury Cocoa Partnership" on January 28th provided a helpful distraction from such problems" means:

a. L'annonce par la société de son « Partenariat Cacao Cadbury » le 28 janvier a été un dérivatif utile à de tels problèmes.

b. L'annonce par la société de son « Partenariat Cacao Cadbury » le 28 janvier a fourni une distraction appréciable pour de tels problèmes.

c. L'annonce par la société de son « Partenariat Cacao Cadbury » le 28 janvier a fait utilement diversion à de tels problèmes.

3. Explain the meaning of water-fetching duties. Decompose the phrase.
4. What other things could the children do when they are liberated from their duties?
5. Ghana provides 70% of Cadbury's worldwide supply. Write the other figures in percentage.

a. Ghana provides all of the cocoa for Cadbury's British operations: Ghana provides......... % of the cocoa for Cadbury's British operations.

b. It buys one-tenth of the crop produced in Ghana: It buys......... % of the crop produced in Ghana.

c. Kuaya Kokoo, Ghana's largest co-operative owns half of Divine Chocolate founded in Britain in 1998: It owns............... % of Divine Chocolate.

d. Fairtrade sales are rocketing in the US and Europe's market grew by a third last year: Europe's market grew by.......% last year.

6. Why don't the children of cocoa farmers want to work in the family business anymore?
7. "But we found that productivity, not price, was the problem" means:

a. The challenge is to cut the farmers' income.

b. They want to increase the average production.

c. Fairtrade cocoa is of little benefit to Ghanaian producers.

8. Pushing out the message whether on their websites and in advertising campaigns, big companies want to tell the world about their good citizenship. (see the chart above) Find an example of this behaviour.
9. Explain the gap between Cadbury's pledge and what Fairtrade thinks it is likely to do. Although Cadbury..........., it is likely to.....................................
10. Do you know any of the companies mentioned in the article? What products do they make?

4 Practice your technical skills

Exercice 18.3

Le commentaire de texte

L'objectif du commentaire est double. Tout d'abord, comme un résumé, il constitue une version abrégée du texte, n'en proposant que les éléments essentiels. Mais cependant, contrairement au résumé, il se place du point de vue du lecteur, et non de l'auteur du document. Il a ainsi pour objectif d'aider le lecteur potentiel à comprendre et interpréter le texte.

Rédigez en anglais un commentaire de l'article, en mettant en avant les difficultés rencontrées par Cadbury et le plan mis en œuvre par le confiseur pour sécuriser son approvisionnement en cacao (vous vous appuierez sur le plan en anglais proposé plus loin).

Qu'est-il souligné à la fin de l'article en ce qui concerne d'une part les autres compagnies et d'autre part Fairtrade ?

Fairtrade est le gardien d'une production durable. Êtes-vous d'accord avec ce qu'ils prônent ?

• Write an introduction in which you indicate:
– the nature of the document (article, advertisement, extract from a book, graph, cartoon, etc.);
– the source (headline, title of newspaper, writer (if well-known), date);
– the theme of the text: what issue does the document deal with?
– its structure: introduce words that help to understand the composition of the article (first, secondly, then, he goes on to say, in conclusion, he concludes with, etc.);
– the writer's approach (i.e. emotional, biased, humorous, sarcastic, satirical, etc.).
• Give a brief description of the text, in which you stress the main points and indicate the connections between them. Let the writer take credit and responsibility for his views (he asserts that, he argues that, he reminds us that, he stresses that, according to the writer, in his opinion, etc.).
• Finally assess the writer's conclusion and his/her approach of the theme, give your own opinion in a few words, say how you feel about the writer's point of view.

Exercice 18.4

La traduction

Traduisez en français les deux derniers paragraphes de l'article.

PARTIE 2

Corrigés des exercices

Corrigé 1.1

1. allegations
2. a sweatshop
3. the Third World
4. to abide by
5. free flow

Corrigé 1.2

1. La croissance économique des deux pays les plus peuplés au monde nous enrichira tous, argumente Tarun Khanna, professeur à l'université d'Harvard.
2. Khanna, homme à la voix calme, qui, pour son livre, a discuté avec des centaines de personnes travaillant dans les affaires ainsi qu'avec des stratèges, offre une vision optimiste de la croissance de l'Inde et de la Chine, qui à elles deux ont une population de 2,4 milliards d'habitants.
3. Dans une démocratie parfois tapageuse, dans laquelle les électeurs votent pour des députés qui ont un casier judiciaire, la tâche du gouvernement est de se désengager et de laisser le secteur privé mener la croissance et créer des emplois.
4. L'approche de la Chine en ce qui concerne le développement économique – basé sur la production et des projets importants d'infrastructure, qui va de la construction de barrages à celle de voies ferrées, ainsi que concernant la politique étrangère est l'exemple type de pouvoir autoritaire.
5. Si cela devait se produire – soit au sujet de Taïwan ou de la péninsule Coréenne ou bien encore au sujet du Tibet ou du Pakistan – cela ne serait pas un problème interne à l'Asie. Le monde entier serait impliqué.

Corrigé 1.3

The BRICKs have fared better than expected in the face of the recession gripping Europe and the United States. They are now accounting for over half of global economic output. Recent figures show economic power is shifting from the developed economies to emerging ones that are becoming major players on the global scene, and changing it.
What's more, until recently a dominant share of Foreign Direct Investment simply went from OECD nation to OECD nation. Now FDI from emerging countries has been on the rise. But emerging markets have also become more important as destinations of FDI, above all from OECD multinationals. These new trends indicate a greater resilience of FDI inflows towards emerging markets and a worse situation for OECD peers.
This forces us to rethink our embedded ideas about global leadership. So what lessons should we take away from all this?
From emerging markets' perspective, the improvements in manufacturing process are not seen as disruptive influences but ingenious attempts of manufacturing industries. From Western viewpoint this seems like something completely new, and a variety of inspiration can be witnessed.
For example, disruptive technology has become a byword for efficiency. While many companies assume that 'disruptive' connotes a highly-sophisticated, high-end product with cutting-edge technology that will appeal to early adopters; disruptive innovations are simpler, cheaper and offer value to the less profitable. They do not appeal to entrenched market leaders because they tend to under-perform existing technologies and serve lower income consumers at the Bottom of the Pyramid.
There is evidence that the shift of consumers away from expensive products is a widespread trend.

Haier is an excellent case in point, inspired by the concept of cheap fridges with bare minimum features, it has created an entirely new category because it has taken the hint of the need to change from passive consumption of throwaway convenience to a way to improve quality of life by saving cost, material and energy and minimizing the impact on the environment.
It seems that disruptive innovations, especially from developing locations in the world, could permeate the way appliances are built for more profitable markets and become the movement of the future for the main players. They provide a less-complicated answer for our true needs. We can't afford to ignore this movement.

Corrigé 2.1

Faux-ami dans le texte : *to achieve* qui signifie « réaliser ».

Corrigé 2.2

Mot	Base	Préfixe	Suffixe	Nature	Traduction
growing	grow		ing	adjective	croissant(e)
effectiveness	effective		ness	noun	efficacité
messier	messy		(i)er	adjective	plus désordonné(e)

Corrigé 2.3

Mot	Formation	Nature	Traduction
downside	down + side	noun	inconvénient
skyscraper	sky + scrape + suffix "er"	noun	gratte-ciel
healthcare	health + care	noun	soins de santé

Corrigé 2.4

Mot	Contexte ou mots connus	Traduction
defective	a defect	défectueux
befitting	to fit	convenable
lifted	a lift = un ascenseur	tirer/sortir/hisser
hinder	downside, lack	gêner/entraver
slums	India, skyscrapers	taudis, bidonvilles

Corrigé 2.5

Mots de liaison		Prépositions	
while	pendant que	*above*	au-dessus de
yet	cependant	*between*	entre
since	depuis	*among*	parmi

Corrigé 2.6

Pronom ou adjectif	Représente
these	*India and China*
its	*General Electric*
his	*Bill Emmot*
who	*Khanna*

Corrigé 2.7

Verbe	Temps	Indication
vote	simple present	habit, something usual
were	simple past	past and completed action, no link with the present

Corrigé 2.8

Auxiliaire modal	Implication
could	hypothesis

Autres modaux :
should/must/have to/need/may/might...

Corrigé 2.9

China's approach to economic development to foreign policy typifies "hard power". India, represents "soft power".
Lorsque vous avez ainsi travaillé sur un texte, vous pouvez ensuite répondre à des questions sur ce texte.

Corrigé 2.10

1. The article refers to a book written by Tarun Khanna, a Harvard Business School Professor. In his book entitled "Billions of Etrepreneurs: How China and India Are Reshaping Their Futures and Yours". He states that India and China's growing economies will benefit the rest of the world.
2. India and China are mentioned. We learn that people have different opinions about these two countries. All the people mentioned in the text don't share the same views about these two economic powers.
3.

	Positive aspects	Negative aspects
China	- sort of capitalism - managed to get a lot of people out of poverty - can build important cities - big infrastructure projects	- defective products - jobs outsourced because of cheaper workforce - lack of clear property rights - lack of democracy
India	- important software industry - brilliant movie industry	- electors vote in for people who may have criminal records - government not strong enough to bulldoze slums

4. No, not everybody shares his opinion. On the one hand the anchorman from CNN, Lou Dobbs, thinks that China presents many downsides. On the other hand, Bill Emmott wrote a book in which he stresses the risks of conflicts between India and China and border countries.

Corrigé 3.1

1. tax haven
2. subsidiary
3. an alter-globalist
4. controversial
5. rock-bottom price

Corrigé 3.2

1. Nombre d'entre eux sont de jeunes diplômés d'universités américaines et certains ont refusé des offres d'emploi d'employeurs très en vue comme Google.
2. Des endroits à bas coût comme l'Europe de l'Est et la Chine pourraient devenir des rivaux redoutables en ce qui concerne la délocalisation d'entreprises multinationales occidentales.
3. Ce gouvernement a introduit des cours d'informatique à l'école. Les entreprises travaillent avec des institutions universitaires pour que les jeunes diplômés aient des compétences en lien direct avec le monde de l'emploi.
4. La Nano est un symbole de l'ingéniosité et de l'esprit d'entreprise en Inde. Elle est seulement vendue cent milles roupies (deux mille cent dollars), elle essaie de toucher une nouvelle classe de clients grâce à une mécanique basique.
5. Beaucoup avaient refusé l'indemnité de l'état alors que celui-ci les avait expropriés en toute hâte pour donner du terrain à l'usine Tata Motors.

Corrigé 4.1

Note de synthèse sur les conséquences variées de la mondialisation en Inde

Today globalisation is on the tip of every tongue. Thanks to outsourcing India's economy has known a real boom in recent years but outsourcing does have many consequences. Some people defend its benefits whereas others only stress the problems deriving from it.

Information technology is one of the fields where Indian workers excel but the car industry plays a big part in the economy of India, too.

As far as IT is concerned, India is the first location for outsourcing and a lot of companies have benefited from globalisation. Their ambition is to get work from the West done in India. IT firms work for numerous important American clients, for example, and employ a great number of employees. Their sales account for an important part of India's GDP.

The car industry is the other force of India with an icon company: Tata Motors. They manufacture the world's cheapest car, the Nano. This car remains a symbol of India's creativity as its manufacturers aim at selling a basic car to new customers.

In spite of all this, some unexpected problems arise. The first one being that India's economy remains mainly agricultural. In West Bengal, farmers have refused the compensation they were offered for their land. This land was going to be used for building a plant by Tata Motors.

It is then difficult for Indian plants and also for foreign ones to expand as they wish.

The second problem India has to face is a labour shortage. Actually a lot of engineers come out of school every year but, in spite of their diplomas, they don't always have the

tailored experience to meet the companies' needs. Consequently some Indian firms need to outsource to other parts of the world. They sometimes also do so because languages other than English may be required or because globalisation has led to an increase in wages and to a stronger currency.
There is no one single effect of globalisation. The Indian economy has benefited from this phenomenon but it needs to tackle the problems involved. The government is fully aware of them and is trying to help companies face them. No doubt India will remain an attractive investment destination in the years to come.

Corrigé 5.1

1. to subsidise
2. a scholarship
3. an applicant country
4. a single currency
5. eurosceptics
6. treaties (a treaty)
7. to take in immigrants
8. a think tank
9. to grant asylum
10. the border

Corrigé 5.2

1. Applicant countries must abide by the Human rights Charter in order to join the European Union.
2. The Lisbon summit took place in 2007.
3. Scholarships are granted to students to ease their mobility.
4. The common foreign policy is devised by all the EU members.
5. Europeans fear globalisation and worry about their jobs.

Corrigé 6.1

A **new** book by a pair of academics from America's Johns Hopkins University finds lots of facts to cheer Europeans up. European consumers (ie, all Europeans when they are shopping) are big winners from globalisation, which has delivered cheap imports, held down inflation and kept interest rates low. Despite the fuss about China and India, the EU's share of world exports rose slightly between 2000 and 2006. What is more, two-thirds of Chinese exports involve foreign brands, a good chunk of which are European. Nor does a "made in China" tag mean big revenues for Chinese firms. **In a recent speech** defending globalisation, the EU trade commissioner, Peter Mandelson, cited a University of California study into who gains when an iPod is sold in America for $299. Only $4 stays in China with the firms that assemble the devices, Mr Mandelson explained. $160 goes to American companies that design, transport and retail iPods. A similar pattern holds for many European products

Résumé

Europeans should be happy as a recent American study found out that Europeans get lots of economical advantages from globalisation. Lately, the EU has benefited from EU's imports and exports from China. Actually an American study mentioned that both Europe and the USA only spend a very small amount of money in China for a product manufactured there.
(58 words)

Corrigé 6.2

Résumé de l'article *Winners and Losers*

According to researchers, ever since the creation of Europe, its citizens have clearly benefited from globalisation. In spite of that politicians have not said so: some have doubts and some even feel it as a threat. Only few people have defended this idea.

In fact Europeans may notice the advantages of globalisation but their main fear is about losing their jobs because of outsourcing.

Europeans should be happy as a recent American book stated that Europeans get numerous economical advantages from globalisation. Lately, the EU has benefited from EU's imports and exports from China. Actually another American study mentioned that both Europe and the USA only spend a very small amount of money in China for a product manufactured there.

People's main worry seems to be about jobs though it should be about efficient workforce. One cannot deny that some jobs are delocalised but most of them remain in European countries.

Thus Europeans' feelings about globalisation seem disproportionate but politicians need to be careful as voters are very sensitive to any loss of jobs. While a lot of jobs were created in the service sector in the European Union, people still don't feel secure.

(194 words)

Corrigé 7.1

1. a laptop
2. a text message
3. a network
4. a web designer
5. to upgrade
6. search engine
7. a spreadsheet
8. wireless
9. a wordprocessor
10. data

Corrigé 7.2

1. Les pirates informatiques volent des données.
2. Les téléphones sans fil sont plus conviviaux.
3. Vous devez posséder un mot de passe pour télécharger ce logiciel.
4. Il faut que j'améliore mon matériel et que j'achète une nouvelle imprimante.
5. Il y a eu une récession des sociétés présentes sur Internet dans les années 80.

Corrigé 8.1

1. une feuille de route
2. pays membres
3. donner du pouvoir, de la puissance, de l'autonomie
4. mécanismes de gouvernance
5. session de clôture

Corrigé 8.2

1. problèmes, questions
2. but
3. parties prenantes
4. tirer parti
5. accentuer, augmenter

Corrigé 8.3

1. The OECD is to work with
developed
and developing countries
and international organisations
to improve policies for *the Internet economy*
and increase international co-operation *on issues* <u>such as cybercrime and security</u>.
2. L'OCDE va travailler avec
les pays developpés
et les pays en voie de développement
ainsi que les organisations internationales
afin d'améliorer les politiques *à l'égard de l'économie Internet*
et d'accroître la coopération internationale *sur des questions* <u>comme la cybercriminalité et la sécurité</u>.

Corrigé 8.4

1. The U.S. may raise their tariffs on oil and textiles.
2. The output rose/went up.
3. Exports were/stood at £60 million.
4. Unemployment stayed the same/remained at last month's level.
5. John Peters denied the rumoured merger.
6. Inflation fell/went down/dropped.
7. Japan will soon mass-produce petrol-free cars.

Corrigé 8.5

1. Merger between Khian Sea and Oileak flounders
2. Radon Tied to Lung Cancer?
3. Mr Thomas MacEnroe: Thousands to Suffer if Car Plant Closes
4. Obama Backs Trade Negotiations as Summit Opens
5. Nestle to Sell Subsidiary?
6. Anders, Grayson Back Graham
7. Egyptian Sentenced in Terrorism Case

Corrigé 8.6

Traduction proposée sur le site de l'OCDE :

L'OCDE propose une feuille de route pour le futur de l'économie Internet

L'OCDE continuera de travailler avec les pays développés et en développement ainsi que les organisations internationales pour améliorer les politiques à l'égard de l'économie

Internet et accroître la coopération internationale sur des questions comme la cybercriminalité et la sécurité.
Les pays membres de l'OCDE, la Communauté européenne et des Ministres du Chili, de l'Égypte, de l'Estonie, de l'Inde, de l'Indonésie, d'Israël, de la Lettonie, du Sénégal et de la Slovénie ont affirmé dans une déclaration leur engagement à travailler ensemble pour stimuler l'innovation, la concurrence et l'investissement dans les technologies de l'information et des communications. Leur but ultime est d'instaurer la confiance dans le futur de l'économie Internet et de le sécuriser.
La Déclaration de Séoul a marqué le point final de la Réunion ministérielle de l'OCDE sur le futur de l'économie Internet, organisée dans la capitale coréenne les 17 et 18 juin 2008.
Les participants sont convenus de la nécessité pour les gouvernements de travailler étroitement avec le secteur privé, la société civile et les experts techniques sur des politiques qui encouragent la concurrence, donnent plus d'autonomie aux consommateurs et les protègent, et développent l'accès à Internet et son utilisation à l'échelle mondiale.
« Cette infrastructure étant devenue vitale pour nos économies et nos sociétés, nous devrions tous nous attacher à élaborer des mécanismes de gouvernance et des politiques plus efficaces et fondés sur des bases plus larges », a déclaré Angel Gurria, Secrétaire général de l'OCDE lors de la session de clôture.
Celui-ci a appelé à une nouvelle approche dans la formulation de ces politiques. « Une approche en réseau, plus décentralisée, pour la formulation de politiques à l'égard de l'économie Internet qui prévoit la participation active des parties prenantes ».
Une décennie s'est écoulée depuis la réunion emblématique sur le commerce électronique tenue par les Ministres de l'OCDE à Ottawa, a-t-il rappelé, « mais nous ne pouvons pas parler de l'importance de l'Internet que tous les dix ans, car c'est une éternité pour le cyberespace ». Il s'est engagé à ce que d'ici trois ans un point soit fait sur les suites données à la Déclaration.
La Déclaration établit une feuille de route pour moderniser les politiques des communications qui ont contribué à faire de l'Internet le moteur économique qu'il est devenu aujourd'hui et faire en sorte que celles-ci facilitent son développement futur. La Déclaration préconise que les pouvoirs publics et les entreprises travaillent ensemble pour tirer un parti plus efficace et plus créatif de la technologie et contribuer ainsi à relever des défis planétaires à long terme, comme le changement climatique.
Durant la session de clôture de la Ministérielle, l'OCDE s'est engagée à améliorer les indicateurs statistiques destinés à mesurer l'utilisation et l'accès à l'Internet et ses réseaux, de manière à disposer de données et d'analyses plus fiables, notamment sur l'impact de l'Internet sur les performances économiques et le bien-être social.
L'OCDE est convenue de travailler étroitement avec les parties prenantes pour améliorer la confiance dans l'Internet, protéger plus efficacement les utilisateurs en ligne et accentuer la lutte contre les cyber-menaces par une coopération transfrontalière renforcée.
L'Organisation analysera également la façon dont les instruments de l'OCDE relatifs à la concurrence, la protection des consommateurs, la vie privée et la sécurité sont mis en œuvre par les gouvernements et les entreprises.

Corrigé 9.1

In 2006, the Office of Fair Trading estimated that in total, banks earned **8.3bn** revenues from Britain's **54m** active personal current accounts every year -more than they make from credit cards and savings accounts **combined**. The OFT threatened banks with greater **regulation** and a full-blown investigation. That gives the lie to any claim that current accounts are free. In a hard-hitting report on the **cornerstone** of the retail finance system, the consumer watchdog found that currently, customers paying charges for unauthorised overdrafts **subsidise** free banking for those in credit and that customers are **unaware** of the charges they face.

Banks make **£2.6bn** from customers having insufficient funds on their accounts, often the result of simple customer mistakes. The banks make a further £4.1bn from **interest on customers' deposits**.

Releasing its report at a time when the banking industry is under intense pressure from the **credit crunch**, the OFT argued that the market does not "**work well** for consumers".

The watchdog's main areas of concern are:

– low level of transparency on overdraft fees;
– complexity of charges;
– customers are unable to control whether they use services for which they pay;
– a significant proportion of customers consistently **incur** charges;
– a perception that switching accounts is complex and **risky**.

Even customers who do not pay overdraft fees are losing out on interest payments on accounts in credit. In 2006, 88% of customers received interest of less than **0.5**% a year from current accounts. Free banking in the UK is a myth. The market is **uncompetitive**. Customers **lack** the information they need to choose better deals, and this in turn weakens the banks' **incentives** to compete for customers.

Despite the growing competition, the continuing **dominance** of the 'big four' proves the old adage that the British are more likely to change their partners than their current account provider.

Corrigé 9.2

2. Around half of all revenue generated by accounts derives from net credit interest income and more than 30% comes from insufficient funds charges.
3. It was approximately £8.3 billion.
5. A significant number of consumers do not know how much they will effectively pay in bank fees or how individual elements in the charging structure will be implemented, either before or after they are incurred.
7. A huge 88 per cent of current accounts paid a tiny annual interest rate below 0.5%.
8. The four established banks representing a combined share of 65 per cent of all current accounts.
10. Until 2000, banks tended to pay less than one per cent interest on money deposited on accounts. In early 2000, however, some challengers introduced higher credit interest rates: over 2% from 2001 to 2007. There is a clear difference between the four established banks and the challengers. Most of all the credit held in accounts provided by the four established banks received a credit rate of 0.5 per cent or less in 2006.

Corrigé 9.3

1. In 2007, there was a rapid rise of 3% in unemployment.
2. The number of people employed in the banking industry fell dramatically from 25,000 to 18,000 between 2006 and 2008.
3. The number of shares traded on the stock market rose by 15 million between November and December.
4. Exports of chemicals remained stable over the last two years.
5. Figures decreased slightly to around 650m in 2005 and levelled off at that number until 2007.
6. The company came out of the red two years ago then there was a significant improvement in profits every year for three years.

7. The company made a considerable loss of £5bn, after which there has been a sharp recovery.
8. Sales dropped by 25% for one year, and then they went down again twice.

Corrigé 9.4

1. The price was increased, and this made sales slump dramatically.
2. The steel production experienced a steady progress.
3. After... there was a continuing boom in sales.
4. A significant loss in market share is likely.
5. There may be a fractional growth of 1-2% in Japan's domestic market.
6. Sales improved rapidly for three years, and then they began to level off.

Corrigé 10.1

1. recipient
2. an ATM
3. wages/salary
4. to lure customers
5. to fill out profiles

Corrigé 10.2

1. Ensuite on tendit l'argent à Mlle (ou Madame) Mendez, banquière du groupe, âgée de 24 ans.
2. Les femmes sont des clientes de la banque Grameen, organisation internationale qui la première accorda des micro-crédits à des créateurs d'entreprises issus du Tiers-monde et qui obtint, avec son fondateur, le Prix Nobel de la Paix en 2006.
3. Mais alors que le système (basé sur la pression des pairs plutôt que sur des garanties pour assurer le remboursement des dettes) se développe harmonieusement partout ailleurs, il n'est pas sûr qu'il réussisse ici et que de si petits montants empruntés permettent effectivement à leurs emprunteurs de sortir de leur pauvreté.
4. La caractéristique remarquable de la banque Grameen réside en des réunions hebdomadaires obligatoires pendant lesquelles les banquiers et les autres membres du groupe dispensent aux emprunteurs des notions de gestion, ces mêmes emprunteurs devant rembourser leur prêt devant la communauté réunie.
5. La banque Grameeen cible ses prêts vers les femmes, arguant qu'elle les estime plus responsables que les hommes et plus à l'aise avec l'esprit de communauté. Jusqu'à maintenant, l'organisation dans le quartier de Queens a seulement prêté à des femmes. Mais elle affirme que, dans ce quartier, elle prêtera de l'argent à des hommes et est consciente qu'une discrimination ne peut être faite sur le sexe des gens.

Corrigé 11.1

Commentaire du texte *Lending Plan Won Prize, but Will it Work here?*

Dans cet article publié le premier avril 2008 dans le *New York Times* sous la plume d'Amanda F. Fairbanks, nous sommes informés de la possibilité de prêt offerte à des femmes pauvres à New-York par la banque Grameen, organisme de micro-crédit.
La banque Grameen a été créée au Bangladesh par Muhammad Yunus en 1976. Elle prête de petites sommes d'argent sans garantie surtout à des femmes. Les montants de ces prêts sont destinés à créer de petites entreprises qui permettent à leurs emprunteurs de sortir de la pauvreté dans laquelle ils se trouvent. Le montant de ces prêts n'est jamais

très élevé et les remboursements se font obligatoirement toutes les semaines sous les yeux des autres membres du groupe d'emprunteurs créant ainsi un sentiment de communauté. Lorsque les remboursements sont terminés, la banque réinvestit la somme de départ vers d'autres emprunteurs du même groupe.

L'expérience, qui a démarré dans des pays en voie de développement tels que le Bangladesh, se poursuit aujourd'hui aux États-Unis avec plus ou moins de bonheur.

Le texte présente ainsi une expérience amorcée à New York, dans le quartier de Queens, où vivent beaucoup d'immigrants. Les montants prêtés restent là aussi faibles et aident des femmes à créer leur propre entreprise – majoritairement des entreprises de services. Les prêts peuvent également servir à sortir certains d'une mauvaise passe. Les entreprises ainsi créées sont un des facteurs qui permettent aux emprunteurs de sortir de la pauvreté extrême dans laquelle ils se trouvent – malheureusement cela ne peut être le seul.

C'est donc une des difficultés rencontrées aux États-Unis, l'autre étant que la pression des pairs (ou membres d'un groupe d'emprunteurs) a moins de sens que dans les pays en voie de développement. Malgré des expériences antérieures parfois négatives et des opinions parfois défavorables, la banque Grameen a pourtant l'intention de les poursuivre dans l'ensemble des États-Unis en les étendant aux hommes sous peine de se voir traiter d'organisation sexiste.

La banque Grameen a d'ores et déjà accordé de nombreux prêts sans garantie à des femmes pauvres dans des pays en voie de développement. Cela a valu à son créateur le Prix Nobel de la Paix en 2006. Il est intéressant de constater que cette banque va continuer son travail dans des pays en voie de développement à l'intention des populations les plus pauvres.

(385 mots)

Corrigé 12.1

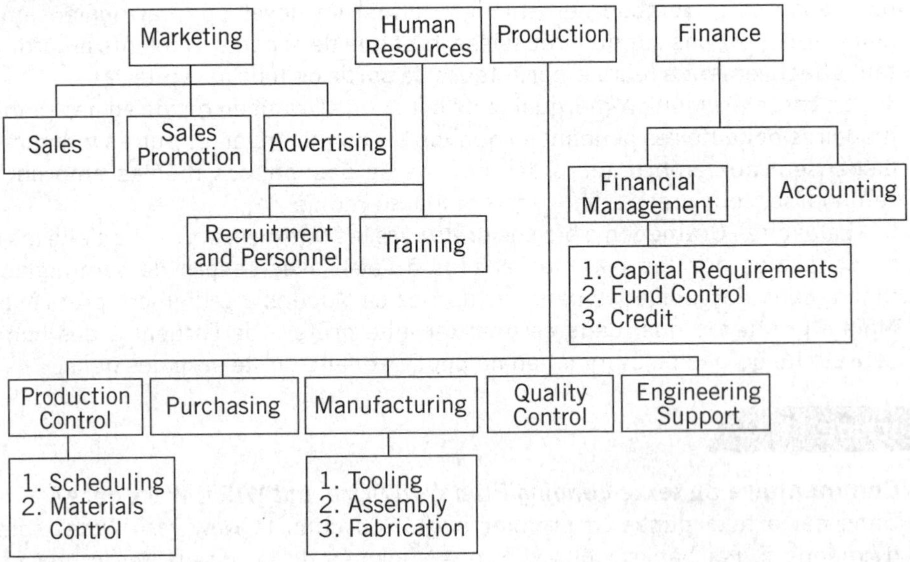

Corrigé 12.2

Mots à conserver :
a. hierarchical
b. traditional
c. functional
d. manufacturing
e. large enterprise
f. simple

Corrigé 13.1

1. Four documents have a letterhead: Ets Magnum (1), BTS (2), O'Shee Pharmaceuticals (5), Publishall CO Ltd (6).
2. Ms for a married or single woman (which does not reveal marital status) if the woman has already used this title when writing to you, Mrs for a married woman, Miss for a single woman or girl.
3. When you don't know the name of the person write Dear Sir/Madam.
4. If you begin Dear Sir or Madam end with Yours faithfully.
5. In a letter that begins Dear Ms Baker, Dear James end with Yours sincerely.
6. Writing to a business associate before closing you can use: With (very) best wishes.
7. encs: enclosures. It means that a document is enclosed with the letter.

incl: including
asap: as soon as possible
pp: per pro (on behalf of) when the letter is signed by someone different from the person who wrote the letter (5).
no: number
plc: public limited company
St: street
Rd: road

Corrigé 13.2

Email 1: Regarding your order
Email 2: Meeting 11/6
Email 3: Shipping confirmation
Email 4: Special Offer!
Email 5: Action re contract

Corrigé 13.3

1. Re your last email...
2. Just a short note to let you know that...
3. Good news!
4. We can confirm that...
5. Sorry for...
6. Unfortunately...
7. Please.../Can you...?
8. Can you...?/Please...?
9. Do you want me to...?
10. Shall I...?
11. I'll get back to you.

12. I've attached...
13. Thanks for your help.w
14. If there's anything else, just let us know.
15. Looking forward to...
16. Regards/Best wishes.

Corrigé 13.4

a) however
b) have slowly
c) by
d) likely
e) improvement
f) although
g) flat
h) forecast
i) will
j) rise steadily
k) be due to
l) even if
m) create
n) even though

Corrigé 13.5

1. Finally/Firstly
2. Furthermore/In addition
3. However/Nevertheless
4. Even though/In spite of the fact that
5. As a result/Therefore
6. Above all/In particular
7. In fact/In reality
8. In conclusion/Taking everything into consideration

Corrigé 13.6

1. A	6. J
2. G	7. B
3. F	8. H
4. E	9. I
5. D	10. C

Corrigé 13.7

1. until – by
2. will – would
3. I'm write – I'm writing
4. attach – attached
5. I'm really – I really
6. at 15 Apr – on 15 Apr
7. informations – information
8. I apologise – I apologise for

9. hearing you – hearing from you
10. more better – better
11. afraid but – afraid that
12. get back me – get back to me.

Corrigé 13.8

From	Angela.Knight@BBA.co.UK
Date	07: 09: 08
To	Nicolas Freeman@Barclays plc.com
CC	All members
Subject	The OFT's survey

Dear members

I've written down some thoughts about the OFT's survey. It is circulated to all members.

The OFT has criticised bank accounts for being too complex and they accused banks of hiding charges at a time when banks are already under pressure from the credit crunch. However, the survey has only looked at revenue and not considered the cost of running a current account.

The market is very competitive and the annual charge figure is slightly contrived, because they pointed out something that we have been saying time and time again, and that is that 80% of customers don't incur fees. If the banks were forced to change the current methods, other fees would be introduced instead.

Moreover, it is very important that the current banking model, which is what customers have asked for, remains free for them.

The fee structure is clear and obvious and it is made clear when we write to customers. Customers can incur charges if they do things without making arrangements first, but do they really want to pay for ATM use, pay for statements, pay for direct debits in this country? Surely people don't.

What is needed is greater transparency and for switching account providers to be made easier.

Let me know what you think.

Regards

Angela Knight

Spokesperson for BBA

Corrigé 14.1

1. bookkeepers
2. management accountants
3. senior accountants
4. internal audit
5. external auditors

Corrigé 14.2

1. shareholder
2. income statement
3. income less expenditure
4. generating or consuming
5. taxable profit

Corrigé 14.3

1. b
2. l
3. k
4. m
5. h
6. a
7. g
8. e
9. d
10. c
11. j
12. i
13. f
14. n

Corrigé 14.4

1c - 2a - 3c - 4b - 5c

Corrigé 14.5

1. borrow
2. cash
3. loan
4. intangible assets
5. accounts receivable
6. deferred liabilities
7. accounts payable
8. reserves

Corrigé 14.6

1. Total assets: 37, 599,000,000: thirty-seven billion, five hundred and ninety-nine million Euros
2. Treasury shares, at cost: 3,146, 000, 000: three billion, one hundred and forty-six million Euros
3. Total assets: 35,599 + 22,617 = 60,216 : sixty billion, two hundred and sixteen million Euros
4. Total equity: 17,336 + 12,060 = 29, 398 : twenty-nine billion, three hundred and ninety-eight million Euros.
5. Increase in retained earnings: 13,870 – 11,123 = two billion, seven hundred and forty-seven million Euros

Corrigé 15.1

1. *Turnover remained constant*
2. Profits declined sharply
3. Sales fell gradually
4. Costs reached a peak
5. Demand rose sharply
6. Overheads levelled off

7. Prices fluctuated
8. Output increased gradually

Corrigé 16.1

1. *to be committed to*	to pledge oneself to	X
2. *to cope with*	X	to adapt to
3. *comprehensive*	complete	X
4. *proceeds*	X	earnings
5. *to reduce*	to cut	X
6. *a deal*	a transaction	X

Corrigé 16.2

1f - 2e - 3i - 4g - 5h - 6j - 7c - 8b - 9a - 10k - 11d

Corrigé 16.3

Shares in Northern Foods started the year at around 87p, and **peaked** at 100p in February, following the announcement that they had completed the sale of non-core businesses. In early spring they **fell** back to 90p and then **fluctuated** over the next two months when they **dropped** even further to 81p, affected by the spiralling prices of ingredients - almost 5% higher than the year before. In April shares **rallied** to 93p before fluctuating again till the end of May when they **plummeted** to 76p. In June the shares gradually **went down** to 60p and they **declined** to a new low of 55p in July and then **firmed** slightly to 60p at the end of the month.

Corrigé 16.4

As part of Northern Foods' battle to improve its performance, the group has gone through a restructuring process. It is now focused on five key markets the biscuit business, ready meals, sandwiches and salads, and puddings, determined that the company should concentrate on those products where it has something unique to offer. After sorting out the problems of its frozen foods division, Northern Foods is trying to regain its focus by improving the chilled section, reinforcing Fox's reputation and launching Goodfella's into the chilled category.
The group's £211.2 million disposal of vast parts of the business represents the first stage of a radical overhaul which helps the group be better positioned for the future. Its Smith Flour Milling, NFT Distribution, Cakes and Speciality Bread and Chilled Pastry products were sold aiming to focus on its key food categories. Eliminating low-margin and low-volume products from their range accounts for 40 per cent of group revenue.
Soaring commodity prices and tough competition have also forced a change of culture at Northern. They are coping with rising food costs by passing the higher costs of ingredients to retailers and simplifying products. This reflects the tension between food producers and retailers as food inflation spirals and consumer spending slows down.
Another virtue of the firm is a confidence to walk away from retail contracts that destroy margins e.g. Northern Foods will stop making some own-brand foods for Marks & Spencer as the deals are unprofitable. It demonstrates that there is a limit to how retailers can squeeze suppliers. But it also shows that the company did not keep the Fenland plant open whatever the human cost – much to the delight of investors. Northern seeks to

reassure the market and insists it will meet market forecasts. For those reasons the group remains a solid hold.

Corrigé 17.1

1a - 2b - 3c - 4c - 5a - 6a - 7b - 8b

Corrigé 17.2

1. The higher oil prices are, the lower the profits.
2. Profits are likely to fall by up to 50%.
3. We would welcome a 12- to-18 month recession.
4. We are not going to see off some of this environmental nonsense unless our economy moves into recession.
5. When the airline slashes prices to maintain demand, profits will be hit.

Corrigé 17.3

1. Les coûts de carburant plus élevés sont partiellement compensés par la faiblesse du dollar.
2. Les actions des transporteurs à bas prix semblent de plus en plus fragiles.
3. Les billets d'avion à bas prix sont gonflés par les suppléments. Ryanair est un de ceux qui s'y adonnent le plus.
4. Le directeur général a fait savoir qu'il espérait qu'une récession éliminerait ses rivaux les plus faibles.
5. Les billets à bas prix ne sont pas aussi concurrentiels qu'auparavant.
6. Le concept de vol ultra- économique de Ryanair signifie les billets les moins chers avec la plus grande ponctualité.

Corrigé 17.4

1. a fifteen-page contract
2. a hundred-dollar bill
3. a three-hour speech

Corrigé 17.5

1. just received
2. sorry
3. confirming
4. unfortunately
5. occurred
6. specified
7. made it clear
8. absolutely vital
9. inconvenience
10. affect
11. don't want
12. consider this acceptable
13. hearing
14. as soon as possible

Corrigé 17.6

4-2-1-5-3

Corrigé 17.7

Dear Sirs
OUR ORDER NUMBER S680
We ordered 200 CDs on 15 March and they were delivered yesterday.
I regret that 20 of them were badly scratched.
The package containing these goods appeared to be in perfect condition and I accepted and signed for it without question. It was on unpacking the compact discs that the damage was discovered. I can only assume that this was due to careless handling at some stage prior to packing.
I am enclosing a list of the damaged goods and shall be glad if you will replace them. They have been kept aside in case you need them to support a claim on your suppliers for compensation.
Yours faithfully
OM

Corrigé 18.1

1. On the one hand you use **fair enough** when you want to say that an action is reasonable to a certain extent, but that perhaps there is more to be said or done: très bien, entendu. On the other hand it means that Cadbury may be dedicated to being fair: être assez juste, assez équitable. The question mark expresses the gap between companies' corporate philanthropy and reality.
2. Cadbury Schweppes cannot afford to ignore its social responsibility in Ghana when it is blamed for its management's behaviour. Now comes consumer's concern over obesity Production has fallen considerably in West Africa, which is a serious difficulty for the company.
3. The headline raises the issue of corporate social responsibility which is now seen as mainstream in big companies such as Cadbury. The question asked is: Are they doing it well?
4. Cadbury's commitment shows a vast range of worthy targets over 10 years. First a fund seed to help West African farmers to increase yields by using fertilisers and by working with each other. Then it will help them by promoting new crops like red peppers and mangoes - grown beneath cocoa trees-. Moreover, Cadbury is to commission 850 water wells that will free women and children from water-fetching duties. Last but not least, Cadbury plans to finance schools and libraries to give Ghanaian children a better education.
5. Companies are not always motivated by philanthropy. They mostly want to tell the world about their good citizenship. Their chief executives queue up at conferences to explain their passion for their new-found commitment to making their firm more ethical. What's more, governments are taking an ever keener interest in promoting corporate responsibility. All this betrays a certain cynicism about fair trade in the profit-hungry world of business.
6. The cocoa crop is an important source of income for Ghanaian growers whose average production has alarmingly declined to 40% of potential yield. It is not fair that West African farmers should get so little. The money, in short, is in chocolate, not cocoa. So, the farmers' children see no future in growing cocoa. All this is giving Cadbury Schweppes cause for concern.
7. Fairtrade demands that farming co-operatives be paid a stable price, above market rates to cover the cost of sustainable production, plus a premium to be invested in community projects. Their challenge is to get all trade conducted according to fairer principles

but their system leaves unaccredited farmers worse off. On the other hand, Cadbury is more focused on modernising farming techniques. They plan to initiate a seed fund and diversify crops associated with cocoa aiming to change the people's attitude. Cadbury gives more flexibility as it uses Fairtrade cocoa.
8. Similarly, Starbuck and Mars tried to create a better product and got involved in social projects.
9. Fairtrade campaigners are often suspicious with new schemes. Their job is to make sure Cadbury's new strategy is about a better financial deal for farming communities and not about boosting their profits.
10. Although the movement to help poor farmers abroad has a strong impact on commerce, some are suggesting that big companies are profiteering from their commitments and use them as a marketing tool to look more ethical. Companies typically allocate small percentage of pre-tax profits to worthy causes because giving something back to the community seems the right thing to do.

Corrigé 18.2

1. The last sentence is a consequence of the sentence before.
2. c. L'annonce par la société de son « Partenariat Cacao Cadbury » le 28 janvier a fait utilement diversion à de tels problèmes.
3. Le nom « duties » est précédé d'un adjectif composé d'un nom et d'un gérondif (verbe + ing) qui fait référence à une activité, celle d'aller chercher de l'eau. Cela signifie : « les devoirs de portage d'eau ».
4. They could work on their father's farm or get an education and learn a new trade.
5. a. Ghana provides 100% of the cocoa for Cadbury's British operations.
   b. It buys 10% of the crop produced in Ghana.
   c. It owns 50% of Divine Chocolate.
   d. Europe's market grew by 33% last year.
6. The children of cocoa farmers won't work in the family business because their fathers' incomes are too low. They see no future in the growing of cocoa beans because the initiatives of big companies are of little benefit to Ghanaian growers. Their parents can't afford to give them a proper education.
7. b. They want to increase the average production.
8. "Mars, the biggest American chocolate-maker, does not sell any Fairtrade products in spite of loud clamouring from campaigners..."
9. Although Cadbury pledges it will support Ghanaian cocoa farmers and their communities, it is likely to focus on its profits.
10. Schweppes is a soft drink division of Cadbury.
Fairtrade is an organisation aiming to give shoppers a guarantee that some of the money they hand over at the checkout is buying some specific social benefit, usually a better financial deal and support for farming communities in developing countries.

Corrigé 18.3

In this article ironically entitled "Fair enough", extracted from *The Economist* Jan 31st 2008, the journalist takes an interest in Cadbury's challenges to secure its cocoa supply from Ghana. The confectioner has to work harder to protect its reputation and, by extension, the environment in which it does business. Like all food companies, Cadbury faces a backlash over growing obesity. At a time when raw materials are rocketing and investors are starting to show more interest. For example, Nelson Peltz fights to involve elements of socially responsible investment. Moreover, it is uncertain how the company will demerge

its fizzy-drinks business in the current tumultuous financial markets.
Cadbury states that its "Cadbury Cocoa Partnership" is a new ten-year investment of £44 million to finance a seed fund so as to show cocoa farmers how to increase yields using fertilisers and by working together and diversifying their sources of income. Championing water wells, financing schools and libraries also promise farmers and their communities a better deal.
The journalist cynically said that all this is largely defensive, especially the idea that it can help to create value. Cadbury comes under attack when it wants to tell the world about its good citizenship. West Africa produces 70% of the world's cocoa, Ghana cocoa supplies are indispensable to Cadbury but growers capture only a tiny fraction of the money.
What actually triggered off the new initiative is the sharp fall of production of Ghanaian cocoa growers and the fact that their children refused to work like their fathers on low incomes. As a result, Cadbury moved toward a social scheme to protect its precious supply and make profit while helping poor farmers. Unlike Fairtrade that promotes a guaranteed price paid directly to the accredited farmers in developing countries, Cadbury developed a similar scheme with more flexibility over the terms.
For both Starbucks and Mars ethical treatment and behaviour seems to be one of the highest priorities and they are very active in supporting social schemes.
However, Fairtrade acts as watchdog on sustainable production issues. It defends small farmers and makes sure the companies do not act illegally or irresponsibly. Cadbury's scheme is under scrutiny. In practice, few big companies can afford to ignore corporate responsibility. "Doing well by doing good" has become a fashionable mantra. Fairtrade blames businesses for eagerly embedding public responsibilities in the core of their operations and it points to a huge gap between traditional corporate aspirations and their actions.

Corrigé 18.4

Cette semaine les membres de la campagne en faveur de Fairtrade – du commerce équitable – ont accordé au projet de Cadbury un accueil réservé. Barbara Crowther de la Fondation Fairtrade à Londres, s'est exprimée dans ces termes : « Nous saluons l'action de Cadbury pour soutenir les cultivateurs de cacao ghanéens et leurs communautés, et nous comptons sur cette société pour qu'elle s'assure que les principes de développement durable et de commerce équitable soient au coeur même de leur action ».
Fairtrade et les grands groupes ne vont pas naturellement de pair. Le mécanisme d'ajustement des prix de Fairtrade est censé mettre les petits producteurs à l'abri des marchés instables de matières premières, du capitalisme du commerce libre où tous les coups sont permis auquel sont liées les grandes multinationales. Mais les entreprises trouvent les moyens d'améliorer le sort des petits fermiers, et de se tailler leur propre réputation, sans cautionner les principes de Fairtrade. De telles stratégies, qui ignorent les principes de Fairtrade sont-elles un rejet des méthodes qu'il préconise ou un hommage équivoque ?

PARTIE 3

Sujets corrigés

SUJET 1

Sujet inédit
La constitution d'espaces économiques régionaux : l'Europe

Durée : 3 heures

Document 1

Long live the Kyoto Protocol

The 15th Conference of the Parties to the UN Framework Convention on Climate Change, which met last month in Copenhagen, is widely considered to have failed.

[…] This failure was widely anticipated. A cynic would wonder why COP15 (1) would succeed where COP14 failed. […] Back in 1994, Scott Barrett showed that stable treaties have either a large number of signatories who commit to very little, or a small number of signatories who commit to more ambitious targets (Barrett 1994). […] Indeed, Brazil, China, India, South Africa and the US ignored the other 188 countries in Copenhagen and agreed their own accord.

What next? Kyoto does not expire, only the targets

The question is what to do now that Copenhagen has failed. The fundamental positions of the main countries involved are unlikely to change much over the next few years, so the next rounds of the negotiations will probably be a repetition of the moves in Copenhagen.

But there is a "plan B". The Kyoto Protocol was initiated in 1997, completed in 2001, and entered into force in 2005. There are two components to the Kyoto Protocol.

- First, some countries have emissions targets for the period 2008-2012.
- Second, there are "international flexibility mechanisms". Importantly, there is no sunset clause (2) in the Kyoto Protocol. The targets will become obsolete in 2013, but the mechanisms will remain in force. The Kyoto Protocol is therefore the default option. The US is the only substantial country that has not ratified it – but it didn't reject it either; the Kyoto Protocol was never put to a vote in the Senate. The US primarily objected to the targets in the Kyoto Protocol, so a ratification after 2012 could be uncontroversial (3).

Is Kyoto enough?

Is the default any good? […]How would one structure international climate policy? A few points condition the answer to this question.

- First of all, it is futile to try and negotiate legally binding targets for sovereign nations.

This is why the Kyoto Protocol has targets for only a minority of countries (the rich ones) and why some of these countries did not ratify the treaty (US) or withdrew after ratification (Canada). The basis for climate policy lies in a domestic demand for climate policy – not in a multilateral agreement or a supranational command.

- Second, unilateral emission reduction is expensive.

Emission abatement increases the cost of energy, and this puts a country at a competitive disadvantage in product and capital markets. A country would therefore hesitate to reduce its emissions if it suspects that other countries would not follow. A country would need to know about the climate policies of its trading partners before it can decide on the stringency (4) of its own policy. International climate policy thus requires a forum through which countries can gain confidence in each other's climate policies. […]

- Third, the costs of emission reduction vary widely between countries.

Roughly, the demand for lower emissions is greater in richer countries, while it is cheaper to reduce emissions in poorer countries. The second element required for international climate policy, therefore, is a mechanism to arbitrage supply and demand (5). The Kyoto Protocol also has "international flexibility mechanisms", through which private and public actors create and trade emission reduction credits, also in countries without emissions targets.

Richard S.J. Tol, 23 January *(abridged)* www. Voxeu.org

Financial adequacy of the Copenhagen Accord

The commitment contained in the Copenhagen Accord is to set up a fast track fund that will consist of $10 billion per year from 2010 to 2012 (totalling $30 billion). If there is sufficient and transparent action towards mitigation (6), developed countries have committed to mobilise, jointly, $100 billion dollars a year by 2020. The mitigation targets are expected to have a substantial impact on global emissions. But they are insufficient to curb emissions below 2005 levels by 2020.

It is thus necessary to invest in the development of low carbon technologies (and their diffusion). With steady emission cuts in the following decades, it would be possible to limit temperature increase to about 2.5°C, above the 2°C threshold but well below the temperature level that would be achieved without strong mitigation action.

Carlo Carraro, Emanuele Masseti, 15 January 2010 *(abridged)* wwwVoxEU.org

(1) *COP 15* : Copenhagen 15

(2) *sunset clause* : *sunset law*, loi en vigueur dans la plupart des états américains selon laquelle les programmes mis en place par le gouvernement doivent être régulièrement réévalués. Donc, ici, pas de réévaluation prévue.

(3) *uncontroversial* : incontestable

(4) *stringency* : sévérité

(5) *supply and demand* : l'offre et la demande

(6) *mitigation* : atténuation

Document 2

How can we reduce greenhouse gas emissions?

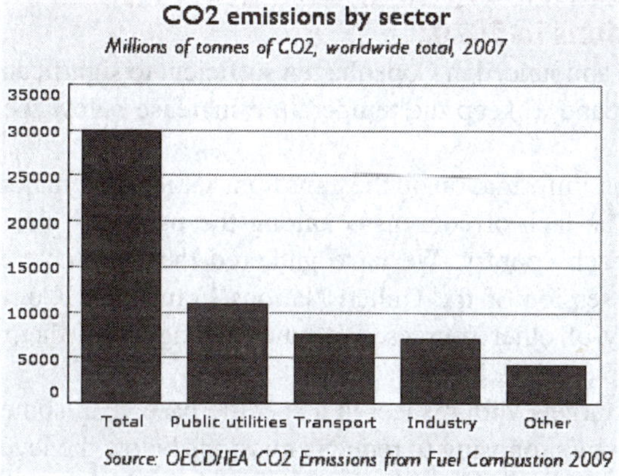

Source: OECD/IEA CO2 Emissions from Fuel Combustion 2009

The OECD argues for a range of policies with an emphasis on putting a price on carbon emissions, e.g. through carbon taxes and a "cap and trade" system in which companies can buy and sell the right to emit a certain amount of greenhouse (1) gases. If a global carbon market is developed over the next decade, it would only cost one-tenth of a percent of average world GDP growth between 2012 and 2050 to keep greenhouse gas concentrations at safe levels. Carbon pricing would need to be complemented by energy efficiency regulations and standards and increased investment in research and development.

Removing environmentally-harmful subsidies to energy consumption and production is an important first step in establishing a price for carbon emissions. Joint OECD-International Energy Agency analysis shows that removing fossil fuel (2) subsidies in emerging economies and developing countries could reduce global greenhouse gas emissions by 10% by 2050.

www.oecd.org/cop 15

(1) *greenhouse* : serre

(2) *fossil fuel* : combustible fossile (pétrole)

Document 3

'And in memory of Copenhagen let's now hear
'Where did our love go ?' by the Three Degrees'

www.CartoonStock.com

Document 4

What is the effect of the announced Copenhagen targets on global greenhouse gas (GHG) emissions in 2020?

Are the domestic abatement plans announced in Copenhagen sufficient to significantly reduce global Green House Gas emissions and to keep the temperature increase below the proposed 2°C target?

The following table summarises our information on the emissions targets that major countries have announced in Copenhagen. The lack of consensus among the parties is clear from the absence of abatement targets for each country. We have gathered the national targets from records of the 18 December 2009 session of the United Nations Framework Convention on Climate Change and from a variety of other sources. We have homogenised them to reflect changes of emissions with respect to (wrt) 1990.

Instead of announcing emissions targets with respect to a specific base year, some countries have taken a more flexible approach by proposing to reduce emissions below the level that they are expected to achieve if climate policy would not be implemented. Such a scenario without any policy to curb emissions is often called the "business-as-usual" (BaU) scenario.

BaU emissions scenarios produced by economy-energy-climate integrated assessment models (IAM) are a good indicator of plausible short-term emissions trajectories.

GT CO2-eq: Gigaton of carbon dioxide equivalent.

Abridged from Two good news from Copenhagen.
Carlo Carraro, Emanuele Masseti,
15 January 2010
wwwVoxEU.org

The Copenhagen emissions reductions commitment

Country	Reduction Target at COP15[5]	Emissions target wrt 1990	GHG Emissions (GT CO2-eq) excluding LULUCF 1990[6]	2005[6]	Committed in 2020[5]	BaU in 2020	Commitment in 2020 wrt BaU in 2020
China[1]	reduce carbon intensity of output by 40-45% wrt 2005	172%	3,72	7,60	10,10	10,10	0%
United States	-17% wrt 2005	-3%	5,99	7,01	5,82	9,25	-37%
Euro 27	-20% wrt 1990[7]	-20%	5,38	5,04	4,30	5,95	-28%
Brazil	-36% wrt BaU	13%	1,61	2,56	1,82	2,84	-36%
Russian Federation	-22% to -25% wrt 1990	-23,5%	3,15	2,32	2,41	2,83	-15%
India[1]	reduce carbon intensity of output by 20-25% wrt 2005	133%	1,38	2,09	3,20	3,20	0%
Indonesia	-26% wrt BaU	64%	0,86	1,57	1,41	1,91	-26%
Japan	-25% wrt 1990	-25%	1,26	1,41	0,94	1,70	-44%
Canada	-20% wrt 2006	-3%	0,58	0,74	0,56	0,89	-37%
South Korea[2]	-4% wrt 2005 or 30% wrt BaU	117%	0,30	0,67	0,65	0,80	-19%
Mexico	-5% wrt BaU	43%	0,48	0,65	0,69	0,72	-5%
Australia	-5% to -25% wrt 1990	-15%	0,46	0,59	0,39	0,68	-43%
South Africa[3]	-34% wrt BaU	5%	0,35	0,44	0,36	0,54	-34%
New Zealand	-10% to -20% wrt 1990	-15%	0,06	0,08	0,05	0,10	-46%
Total Major Emitters		*28%*	*25,57*	*32,78*	*32,71*	*41,50*	*-21%*
Rest of the World[4]	Business as Usual	29%	11,73	12,64	*15,17*	15,17	20%
World		*28%*	*37,30*	*45,43*	*47,89*	*56,67*	*-16%*

[1] We used the increment of GHG emissions in the WITCH model Business as Usual scenario because the committed reduction of carbon intensity is inferior to the BaU autonomous carbon intensity improvement.

[2] According to estimates based on the WITCH model BaU the emissions target of South Korea would be 5.52 GT CO2-eq in 2020 if the -30% wrt BaU is implemented; here we use the less stringent target of -4% wrt 2005.

[3] A 25% increment of emissions in the BaU has been assumed extrapolating South Africa from a wider regional aggregate in the WITCH model.

[4] The average growth rate of emissions has been extrapolated from WITCH model Business as Usual scenario.

[5] Emissions targets have derived from a variety of sources. They have all been computed with respect to all GHGs emissions.

[6] IEA CO2 Emissions from Fuel Combustion - Emissions of CO2, CH4, N2O, HFC, PFC, FS6 Vol 2009 release 01.

[7] The EU has agreed to cut emissions by 30% wrt 1990 if other developed nations follow suit.

Lisez attentivement les 4 documents précédents.

Compréhension

Exercice 1.1

Vous rédigerez *en français* une note de 250 mots (+ ou – 10%) qui fera ressortir les points positifs et la cohérence de l'accord de Copenhague.

Expression en anglais

Exercice 1.2

Traitez *en anglais* les questions suivantes.

a. Say what point of view is illustrated in document 3 (120 Words +/– 10%).

b. Look at the table in document 4 and answer the following questions
- What intensity targets did China and India announce?
- What would be the Copenhagen commitments for the biggest emitters as a group?
- What would those countries' emissions be on a business-as-usual scenario?

Exercice 1.3

Vous êtes Susan Firth, chargée d'études (*researcher*) au service communication de l'*UN Framework Convention on Climate Change* et vous effectuez une recherche sur ce qui motive la prolifération des conférences ayant pour thème : *le changement climatique dans le monde depuis la fin de Copenhague 15.*

On vous demande de rédiger un courrier électronique *en anglais* adressé au directeur du service de la communication du *Fourth Assessment Report of the Intergovernmental Panel on Climate Change*. C'est Cliff Broom, un ancien collègue. Il s'agit d'un court résumé du contenu de votre rapport.

Utilisez les informations contenues dans les quatre documents fournis et vos propres arguments pour éveiller son intérêt sur les points suivant :
- Les causes de la prolifération des réunions et conférences ;
- Les principaux arguments soulevés lors des différentes réunions.

Vous joindrez à ce mail des documents illustrant votre recherche.

(180 words +/– 10%)

Corrigé 1.1

Bien que la Conférence de Copenhague soit unanimement perçue comme un échec, elle restera dans l'histoire comme l'événement qui a redéfini le nouveau monde multipolaire et annoncé une époque de transition dans les relations internationales. Si, comme le dit Scott Barrett, les traités signés par un petit nombre (ici 5 pays) sont ceux dont les objectifs sont les plus ambitieux, alors cet accord l'est forcément puisqu'il ignore les 188 autres participants.
Le sommet de Copenhague, s'il n'a pas atteint les objectifs élevés qu'il s'était fixés, a du moins le mérite d'être à l'origine d'une déclaration d'objectifs nationaux de réduction d'émissions pour 2020. Les dirigeants des principales économies mondiales ont effectivement annoncé leurs objectifs d'émissions, ce qui est très révélateur sur leurs politiques climatiques à venir. Ce sont de bons indicateurs des trajectoires plausibles d'émissions à court terme.
Le deuxième volet positif de l'accord est l'affectation d'un fonds de 30 milliards de dollars sur 3 ans, destiné à combler le fossé entre les objectifs et la réalité.
Copenhague est à l'origine de la définition des ressources qui seront transférées aux pays en voie de développement pour leur faciliter l'accès aux technologies susceptibles de favoriser et maintenir des actions d'atténuation et d'adaptation. Si les actions menées en vue de la réduction des émissions paraissent à la fois suffisantes et transparentes, les pays riches se sont engagés à mobiliser conjointement 100 milliards de dollars par an d'ici 2020.
Les objectifs de modération d'émissions issus du sommet de Copenhague auront un fort impact sur les émissions terrestres sans pour autant les diminuer au-dessous des niveaux de 2005 d'ici 2020, seuil garantissant un recul du réchauffement planétaire.

Corrigé 1.2

a. The cartoon RADIO REAL 6 by Mike Turner is a funny caricature designed to denounce the tentative deal on global warming that became known as the Copenhagen Accord at the end of a two-week diplomatic deadlock and bickering between rich countries and the big emerging economies with neither bloc dominant nor united enough to prevail. This is illustrated by the title of the song: "Where did our love go?"

The title of the cartoon is a pun in itself, indicating that the agreement was signed by the happy few e.g. Brazil, China, India, South Africa and the United States, when most countries were conspicuously absent from the room. The broadcaster uses the phrase "in memory of" which means he talks about someone who has died, in other words, the conference's failure symbolises the demise of the participants' hope. The group's name "The Three Degrees" is also humorous since the main goal of the conference was to significantly reduce global green house gas emissions to keep the temperature increase below the proposed 2°C target.

b. Table Document 4

• **What intensity targets did China and India announce?**

China and India announced they would reduce their carbon intensity by 40%-45% and 20%-25% respectively.

• **What would the Copenhagen commitments be for the biggest emitters as a group?**

As a group, the Copenhagen commitments for the biggest emitters would imply a 28% increase of emissions above the 1990 level.

• **What would those countries' emissions be on a business-as-usual scenario?**

Compared with the business-as-usual scenario for those countries, emissions would be reduced by 21%.

Corrigé 1.3

Écrire un courrier électronique

From Susan.firth@UNFCCC.php
Date: 22.04.10
To CliffBroom@ARIPCC.org
CC
Subject: Summary of report on latest conferences on climate change
Dear Cliff
I hope you're well.

This is a short summary of our research on the after-Copenhagen conferences. You know that since the COP 15 Accord many environment conferences have been held to debate climate change in preparatory meetings to work out a new agreement in time for the next summit in Mexico.

• Background

The talks were triggered by some delegates concerned that the whole process could collapse, given the divisions and the international breakdown on trust. They feel that the only thing that can save mankind from a climate tragedy is the exercise of global democracy.
Actually, the Copenhagen accord is considered useful, but with no legal status it cannot be used to impose other countries' will on the rest of the world, especially by a country that was party to the Kyoto protocol and never ratified it.
Moreover, developing countries are adamant that the UN climate convention is the right forum for negotiating a global deal that includes further emissions reductions under the Kyoto Protocol. Unfortunately richer countries resist this, which leaves no chance on agreeing even a framework.

• The organisers' recommendations

They want more openness and no more secret discussions as during Copenhagen 15.
They are aware of the need for binding constraint to limit global warming to below 2°.
They think that, contrary to traditional UN binding agreements, COP 15 is too weak to compel the worst polluters to comply.

Finally, the participants want to further the UN 20-year process and propose monitoring of progress on national emissions to ensure transparency and accountability.
In sum, there may be too many agendas around the world for their action to ever work. But they look forward to working with Mexico and the broader international community, ideally to establish a legally-binding agreement for post-2012 action under the UNFCCC by the 16th Conference of Parties (COP16).
Please find attached 4 columns dealing with the latest conferences.
If you'd like more details, just let me know.
I look forward to receiving your opinion on this study.
Best wishes
Susan

SUJET 2

Annales corrigées
La globalisation des marchés

Session 2009 — **Durée : 3 h – Coefficient 1**

Aucun matériel (agendas, calculatrices, traductrices…) ni dictionnaire n'est autorisé.

Document 1

Document 2

***The Independent* – Multinationals make billions in profit out of growing global food crisis**

By Geoffrey Lean

Sunday, 4 May 2008

The prices of wheat, corn and rice have soared over the past year driving the world's poor – who already spend about 80 per cent of their income on food – into hunger and destitution.

The World Bank says that 100 million more people are facing severe hunger. Yet some of the world's richest food companies are making record profits. Monsanto last month reported that its net income for the three months up to the end of February this year had more than doubled over the same period in 2007, from $543m (£275m) to $1.12bn.

The Food and Agriculture Organisation reports that 37 developing countries are in urgent need of food. And food riots are breaking out across the globe in many developing countries.

Benedict Southworth, director of the World Development Movement said that the benefits of the food price increases were being kept by the big companies, and were not finding their way down to farmers in the developing world. […]

The revelations are bound to increase outrage over multinational companies following last week's disclosure that Shell and BP between them recorded profits of £14bn in the first three months of the year – or £3m an hour – on the back of rising oil prices.

(Abridged)

Document 3

Professor explores turning poor people into consumers
University of Michigan – Record online

By Bernie DeGroat

Four billion people around the world live on less than $2 a day, but these poorest of the poor represent the potential for one of the most vibrant growth markets in the world, says a Business School professor.

C.K. Prahalad argues that private-sector businesses can help alleviate **(1)** poverty and, at the same time, make a profit by turning the poor—those at the bottom of the economic pyramid—into consumers and developing viable markets for innovative products and services in under-served and long-neglected areas.

"What is needed is a better way to help the poor," says Prahalad, professor of corporate strategy and international business. "A way that involves motivated participants on both ends and incorporates innovation to achieve sustainable win-win scenarios where the poor are empowered and the companies providing products and services to them make a profit."

Such a way, he says, already exists and has gone well past the idea stage as private enterprises have begun to successfully build markets at the bottom of the pyramid **(2)** as a way of eradicating poverty.

(Abridged)

(source : www.ur.umich.edu/0405/Sept13_04/10.shtml)

(1) make less severe
(2) low income consumers

Document 4

Profiting from the Poor? Considerations for Investing at the Base of the Pyramid

Developing countries play a growing role in the global economy. A 2008 KPMG **(1)** International survey shows that companies plan to invest heavily in so-called emerging markets, mainly at the expense of developed economies like the US and Japan

Introduction

Access to new consumers is a deciding factor in these companies' investment choices. And although discussions about emerging markets often centre on large economies such as China and Brazil, many companies are looking more broadly at the developing world that represents over 80 percent of the world's population. This trend is driven by two factors. Firstly, developed country markets are increasingly saturated, while many "new and emerging markets" have experienced impressive rates of growth. Secondly, although economic development has by no means been universal and widespread poverty persists in many countries, millions of consumers in the developing world have for the first time the spending power that puts processed and branded products and services within their reach.

Conclusion

Saturated Western markets are increasingly encouraging companies to look towards the 80 percent of the world's population that live in developing countries as a source of further growth. However, while the aspirations of consumers in developing countries may be similar to those of Western consumers, many of them live near or in poverty and have fundamentally different needs. Moreover, the business environment can be challenging to say the least. It is by no means clear whether large (Western) companies are able to make a profit in low-income markets. Indeed, some companies will conclude that their products and capabilities are not suited to these markets and focus on Western consumers and the richer segments in developing countries. Others will attempt to serve consumers on lower incomes. The challenges inherent in doing so should not be underestimated, while any commitment to BoP **(2)** markets should be solid and consistent. Companies that do succeed in low-income markets can unlock a huge potential for profits. There may be a social dividend, too, if companies develop products and services that have a positive impact on consumers' social and economic development.

Source : KPMG report "Sustainable Insight". October 2008

(1) KPMG : one of the largest auditing firms.
(2) BoP : Base/Bottom of the Pyramid: low income consumers.

▸ **Travail à faire**

Le dossier qui vous est proposé comporte 4 documents :
- **Document 1** : la couverture d'un ouvrage intitulé *Make Poverty Business*, publié en octobre 2006.
- **Document 2** : un article de *The Independent* du 4 mai 2008 intitulé : *Multinationals make billions in profit out of growing global food crisis.*
- **Document 3** : un extrait d'un article publié sur le site de l'université du Michigan : *Professor explores turning poor people into consumers.*
- **Document 4** : l'introduction et la conclusion du rapport d'octobre 2008 de KPMG : *Profiting from the Poor? Considerations for Investing at the Base of the Pyramid.*

Compréhension (10 points)

Exercice 2.1

Vous rédigerez *en français* une note de 250 mots (+ ou – 10%) qui mettra en évidence les stratégies les plus efficaces que les entreprises doivent mettre en œuvre pour réussir durablement dans les pays en voie de développement.

Expression en langue anglaise (10 points)

Vous rédigerez *en anglais* les deux exercices suivants.

Exercice 2.2

Say if these two documents (a and b) illustrate the same point of view about helping poor countries and justify your answer (150 words +/- 10%).

a) **Cartoon**: SAFE MONEY

Source : www.terra-economica 10/06/04 Remy Geasse.

b) **Diagram**: *Strategy for Companies willing to Invest in BoP Markets*

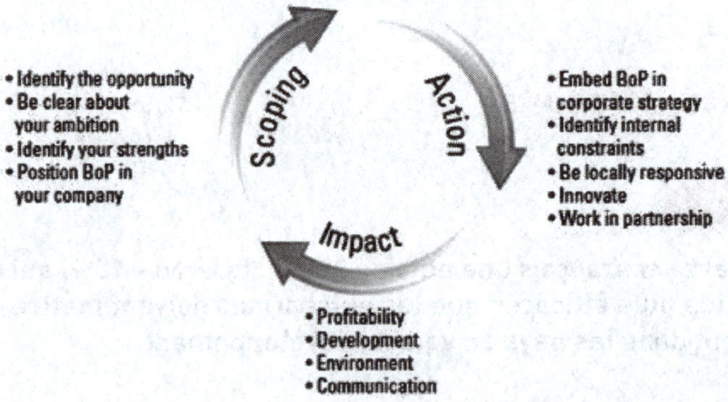

Source : KPMG report.

Exercice 2.3

Vous travaillez au service communication du *World Developement Movement* et vous êtes chargé de rédiger un courrier électronique développant un argumentaire (au moins trois arguments) adressé au président d'une multinationale de votre choix pour le convaincre d'investir efficacement dans les pays en voie de développement.

Pour formuler vos conseils (au moins trois conseils), vous pouvez vous appuyer sur le schéma *Strategy for Companies willing to invest in BoP markets*, sur l'ensemble du dossier et/ou sur vos connaissances personnelles (150 mots +/– 10%).

Corrigé 2.1

Face à la saturation des marchés, les grandes entreprises prennent conscience que les 4 milliards de pauvres situés au bas de la pyramide représentent un potentiel de marché considérable. Leur pouvoir d'achat individuel est faible (moins de $2), mais leur grand nombre offre des opportunités de marché non négligeables, un moteur d'innovation et de croissance économique future. Certains pays émergents où des millions de consommateurs disposent pour la première fois d'un pouvoir d'achat qui met les produits industriels et de marque à leur portée, connaissent des taux de croissance impressionnants et les marchés des revenus bas génèrent des bénéfices énormes.
Pour développer ces opportunités efficacement, les entreprises doivent améliorer leur ouverture et leur capacité à collaborer avec les ONG et les gouvernements locaux dans une stratégie globale. Elles doivent adapter produits et services pour permettre aux nouveaux consommateurs d'y accéder et encourager des partenariats stratégiques pour vendre des produits adaptés en créant des profits défiant le court-termisme dominant et en rendant les marchés durables.
Diverses entreprises inventent des alternatives dont le microcrédit, le partenariat Danone-Grameen (vente de yaourts enrichis à prix abordable au Bangladesh), l'auto-construction de logement, les pompes à eau manuelles pour l'Afrique et tentent de diminuer les prix sans nuire à la qualité des produits grâce à des innovations techniques, des changements de format, ou en jouant sur l'effet volume.
Les stratégies de marketing sont révisées avec des produits à faible budget et usages spécifiques : les shampoings efficaces à l'eau froide, les emballages de petite taille, ou les produits vendus à l'unité. Les PPP, (Produits à positionnement populaire) de Nestlé trouvent désormais leur marché en France à cause de la crise économique
Il faut passer des grands centres commerciaux aux petites boutiques, aux stands de rue, engager la lutte contre les intermédiaires corrompus par l'introduction d'internet permettant aux agriculteurs le contrôle des prix de vente de leur produit.
Il faut mettre en place des architectures sociales et technologiques tournées vers la « co-création » et les scénarios gagnant-gagnant adoptant de nouveaux modes d'organisation plus horizontaux qui placent l'entreprise en permanence à l'écoute des expériences, des remarques des consommateurs pour permettre l'émergence de nouvelles réponses à l'immense pauvreté.

Corrigé 2.2

The Safe Money cartoon shows us a banker giving money to somebody well dressed while thin hands are holding collection tins. The banker's empty hand means that there is nothing for the poor, while those who already have lots will be given more: it is "safer" to give to the rich, and we are reminded that money is kept in "safes".
On the other hand, the diagram is an illustration of a marketing strategy where companies willing to invest in BoP markets could find ways of working together with poor countries.
There are many suggestions, including being locally responsive, knowing what your company can offer, and evaluating the impact on profitability, development, and the environment.
There are two different approaches here to helping poor countries: either do nothing, as in the cartoon, or try to increase their prosperity in a win-win situation, as in the diagram.
It is not the same point of view.
(153 words)

Corrigé 2.3

From: sandrapearce-worlddevelopment@btnet.uk
To: johnjones-internationalgoodscorp@yahoo.com
Re: investing in BoP markets
Dear CEO,
Your corporation should benefit from investing in poorer countries because
– it's a large source of potential customers, 80% of world population;
– helping poor people will enhance your corporation's image;
– you could benefit both your corporation and your future customers by mutual growth, your profits can increase while poor people become more prosperous;
– if you play a role in the development of emerging countries, you can be pioneers in the field of sustainable development.
If you decide to invest in this programme, you should:
– be clear about your ambition and strengths
– work in partnership with local people
– identify problems, such as cultural differences, beforehand
– invest only in environmentally-friendly projects
– be committed to improving the welfare of future customers
I hope this is of interest to you, and I look forward to hearing from you.
Best regards,
Sandra Pearce, World Development Movement
(147 words)

ANNEXES

- Le référentiel du DCG 12 - Anglais appliqué aux affaires
- Liste des abréviations
- L'Union européenne
- Les faux amis
- Les erreurs les plus fréquentes
- Les fautes d'orthographe à éviter
- L'anglais britannique et l'anglais américain
- La presse britannique et américaine

Le référentiel du DCG 12 - Anglais appliqué aux affaires

Durée : 3 heures.
Coefficient : 1.
12 crédits européens.

▸ Thèmes économiques et sociaux

- Les chocs pétroliers et leurs conséquences
- Les traits contemporains des échanges internationaux
- La place des firmes multinationales
- La globalisation des marchés
- La constitution d'espaces économiques régionaux (Union européenne, ALENA)
- La montée en puissance des pays asiatiques
- Les technologies de l'information et de la communication
- L'aménagement du temps de travail
- L'évolution de la protection sociale
- La concurrence et le droit

▸ L'entreprise

- Les formes juridiques de l'entreprise (française)
- L'organisation de l'entreprise
- Les grandes fonctions de l'entreprise
- Les partenaires de l'entreprise (fournisseurs, clients, banques)
- La création d'entreprise
- La stratégie de l'entreprise
- L'analyse des performances de l'entreprise
- La communication interne et externe de l'entreprise

Indications complémentaires

Le candidat doit montrer une connaissance suffisante de la langue (niveau B2 du cadre commun de référence) pour :

- comprendre et commenter, en anglais, des documents de la vie des affaires tels que des textes, graphiques et tableaux tirés de revues ou d'un rapport annuel d'entreprise ;
- rédiger une note de synthèse, en français ou en anglais, à partir de documents en anglais concernant la vie des affaires ;
- rédiger, en anglais, un document commercial de base (lettre, devis, bon de commande).

Le cadre européen commun de référence pour les langues :
http://eduscol.education.fr/cid45678/le-cadre-europeen-commun-reference-pour-les-langues.html

Liste des abréviations

(The list of abbreviations)

Abréviation en anglais *(abbreviation in English)*	**Signification** *(meaning)*	**Abréviation en français** *(abbreviation in French)*	**Signification** *(meaning)*
AGL	Annual General Meeting	AG	Assemblée Générale annuelle
A levels	Advanced Levels		Équivalent du Baccalauréat français
a.m. (ante meridiem)	in the morning		Du matin
asap	as soon as possible		Aussitôt que possible
ASEAN	Association of South-East Asian Nations	ANASE	Association des Nations d'Asie du Sud Est
Attn	Attention		À l'attention de
B2B	Business to Business		Transaction inter entreprises
B2C	Business to Consumer		Transaction entre entreprises et particuliers
BBC	British Broadcasting Corporation		Organe de programmes de radio et de télévision britannique
BC	Before Christ	Av. J.-C.	Avant Jésus-Christ
bl	barrel		Baril
bn	billion		Milliard
BT	British Telecom		Télécommunications britanniques
C2C	Consumer to Consumer		Transaction entre particuliers
CAD	Computer Assisted Design	CAO	Conception Assistée par Ordinateur
CAP	Common Agricultural Policy	PAC	Politique Agricole Commune
CBI	Confederation of British Industry	MEDEF	Mouvement des Entreprises de France
CEO	Chief Executive Officer	PDG	Président Directeur Général
CIA	Central Intelligence Agency		Surveillance du Territoire
CIF	Cost, Insurance and Freight	CAF	Coût, assurance et fret
Co	Company		Compagnie
COD	Cash On Delivery		Envoi contre-remboursement
CPA	Certified Public Accountant		Expert comptable
CPU	Central Processing Unit		Unité Centrale
CSR	Corporate Social Responsibility	RSE	Responsabilité Sociétale des Entreprises
CV	Curriculum Vitae	CV	Curriculum Vitae
CWO	Cash With Order		Paiement à la commande
Dr	Doctor		Docteur

Abréviation en anglais *(abbreviation in English)*	**Signification** *(meaning)*	**Abréviation en français** *(abbreviation in French)*	**Signification** *(meaning)*
DTI	Department of Trade and Industry		Ministère du Commerce et de l'Industrie
ECB	European Central bank	BCE	Banque Centrale Européenne
EEC	European Economic Community	CEE	Communauté Économique Européenne
EFTA	European Free Trade Association	AELE	Association Européenne de Libre Échange
e.g. (exempli gratia)	for example		Par exemple
EMS	European Monetary System	SME	Système Monétaire Européen
Enc(s)	Enclosure(s) Enclosed	PJ	Pièces jointes
ERASMUS	European Action Scheme for the Mobility of University Students		Programme d'échange d'étudiants et d'enseignants entre les universités et les grandes écoles européennes
EU	European Union	UE	Union européenne
FAO	Food and Agriculture Organisation		Organisation des nations unies pour l'alimentation et l'agriculture
FBI	Federal Bureau of Investigation		(Bureau Fédéral d'investigation)
FDA	Food and Drug Administration		Office du contrôle Pharmaceutique et Alimentaire
FDI	Foreign Direct Investment	IDE	Investissement Direct à l'étranger
FOB	Free On Board		Franco à bord
FTA	Free Trade Area		Zone de libre échange
FTSE	Financial Times Stock Exchange		Entreprise spécialisée dans le calcul et la diffusion d'indices boursiers
GATT	General Agreement on Tariffs and trade		Accord général sur les tarifs et le commerce
GB	Great Britain		la Grande-Bretagne
GCSE	General Certificate of Secondary Education		Certificat général de l'enseignement secondaire (équivalent du DNB : Diplôme National du Brevet)
GDP	Gross Domestic Product	PIB	Produit Intérieur Brut
GM	General Manager		Directeur Général
GM(O)	Genetically Modified (Organisms)	OGM	Organismes génétiquement modifiés
GMT	Greenwich Mean Time		Heure GMT
GNP	Gross National Product	PNB	Produit National Brut
GP	General Practitioner		Médecin généraliste
HCR	High Commissioner for Refugees		Haut Commissariat aux Réfugiés

Abréviation en anglais *(abbreviation in English)*	**Signification** *(meaning)*	**Abréviation en français** *(abbreviation in French)*	**Signification** *(meaning)*
HR	Human Resources	RH	Ressources Humaines
IASB	International Accounting Standards Board		Bureau des standards comptables internationaux
IBM	International Business Machines Corporation		
i.e.(id est)	that is to say		C'est-à-dire
IFRS	International Financial reporting Standards		Normes internationales d'information financière
ILO	International Labour Organisation	OMT	Organisation Mondiale du travail
IMF	International Monetary Fund	FMI	Fonds Monétaire International
incl	including		ci-inclus
IOU	I Owe You		Reconnaissance de dettes
ISO	International Standard Organisation		Organisation des normes internationales
IT	Information Technology		Technologies de l'information
ICT	Information and Communication Technology	TIC	Technologies de l'information et de la Communication
Inc	Incorporation (Incorporated)		Type de compagnie
£	pound		Livre sterling
LAN	Local Area Network		Réseau local
lb	pound		Livre (poids : 450 grammes)
LCD	Liquid Crystal Display		Affichage à cristaux liquides
Ltd	Public Limited Company	SA	Société Anonyme
MBA	Master of Business Administration		Maîtrise de gestion
MD	Managing Director	PDG	Président Directeur Général
Miss	Miss		Mademoiselle
MNC	Multinational Corporation		Multinationale
MoT	Minister of Transport		Ministère des transports
MP	Member of Parliament		Parlementaire
mph	miles per hour		miles par heure
Mr	*Mister*	M.	Monsieur
Mrs	*Missis*	Mme	Madame
Ms	*Miz*		Madame ou mademoiselle
NAFTA	North American Free Trade agreement	ALENA	Accords de Libre Échange Nord Américain
NASA	National Aeronautics and Space Administration		Agence nationale de l'aéronautique et de l'espace

Abréviation en anglais *(abbreviation in English)*	**Signification** *(meaning)*	**Abréviation en français** *(abbreviation in French)*	**Signification** *(meaning)*
NASDAQ	National Association of Securities Dealers Automated Quotations		Association nationale américaine des agents de change
NATO	North-Atlantic Treaty Organisation	OTAN	Organisation du Traité de l'Atlantique Nord
NGO	Non Governmental Organisation	ONG	Organisation Non Gouvernementale
NHS	National Health System		Sécurité Sociale
NIC	Newly Industrialised Country	NPI	Pays Nouvellement Industrialisé
NVQ	National Vocational Qualification		Qualification professionnelle
NYSE	New York Stock Exchange		Bourse de New York
OECD	Organisation for Economic Cooperation and Development	OCDE	Organisation de Coopération et de Développement Économique
OPEC	Organisation of Petroleum Exporting Countries	OPEP	Organisation des Pays Exportateurs de Pétrole
PA	Personal Assistant		Assistante de direction
PAYE	Pay As You Earn		Impôts retenus à la source
PC	Personal Computer		Ordinateur
PDA	Personal Digital Assistant		PC de poche
PLC	Public Limited Company	SARL	Société à Responsabilités Limitées
p.m. (post meridiem)	in the afternoon		De l'après-midi
PM	Prime Minister		Premier Ministre
PO box	Post Office Box	BP	Boîte Postale
pp (per pro)	on behalf of		De la part de
P&P	Postage and Packing		Frais d'expédition
PR	Press Release		Communiqué de Presse
PR	Public Relations		Relations publiques
PTO	Please Turn Over	TSVP	Tournez s'il vous plaît
pw	per week		Par semaine
R&D	Research and Development		Recherche et Développement
RAM	Random Access Memory		Mémoire (RAM)
ROM	Read Only Memory		Mémoire (ROM)
Rd	Road		Route
Ref	Reference		Référence
RRP	Recommended Retail Price		Prix de détail conseillé
$	Dollar		Dollar

Abréviation en anglais *(abbreviation in English)*	**Signification** *(meaning)*	**Abréviation en français** *(abbreviation in French)*	**Signification** *(meaning)*
SCSC	Software and Computing Services Company	SSII	Société de Services en Ingénierie Informatique
SECc	Security and Exchange Commission		Commission (américaine) des échanges en bourse
SIB	Securities and Investment Board		Commission (britannique) des échanges en bourse
SME	Small and Medium Sized Enterprise	PME	Petites et Moyennes Entreprises
SMI	Small and Medium Sized Industries	PMI	Petites et Moyennes Industries
SMS	Short Message Service		Texto
St	Street		Rue
UK	United Kingdom		Royaume-Uni
UNO	United Nations Organisation	ONU	Organisation des nations unies
URL	Uniform Resource Locator		Adresse internet
USA	United States of America		États-Unis d'Amérique
VAT	Value added Tax	TVA	Taxe sur la Valeur Ajoutée
VIP	Very Important Person		
WAN	Wide area Network		Réseau étendu
WHO	World Health Organisation	OMS	Organisation Mondiale de la Santé
WTO	World Trade Organisation	OMC	Organisation Mondiale du Travail
WW	World War		Guerre mondiale
WWW	World Wide Web		Toile mondiale
Y2K	Year two thousand		An 2000

L'Union européenne

(European union)

► **Pays et nationalités** *(Countries and nationalities)*

En français, seuls les noms de nationalité prennent une majuscule, les adjectifs n'en prennent pas. En anglais, noms et adjectifs prennent des majuscules.

Pays *(country)*	**Capitale** *(capital)*	**Langue officielle** *(official language)*	**Habitants** *(people)*	
			Singulier *(singular)* *a/an*	**Pluriel** *(plural)* *the …*
Austria	Vienna	German	Austrian	Austrians
Belgium	Brussels	French / Dutch / German	Belgian	Belgians
Bulgaria	Sofia	Bulgarian	Bulgarian	Bulgarians
Cyprus	Nikosia	Greek / Turkish	Cypriot	Cypriots
the Czech Republic	Prague	Czech	Czech	Czechs
Denmark	Copenhagen	Danish	Dane	Danes
Estonia	Tallinn	Estonian	Estonian	Estonians
Finland	Helsinki	Finnish	Finn	Finns
France	Paris	French	Frenchman	French
Germany	Berlin	German	German	Germans
Greece	Athens	Greek	Greek	Greeks
Ireland	Dublin	English / Irish	Irishman	Irish
Italy	Rome	Italian	Italian	Italians
Latvia	Riga	Latvian	Latvian	Latvians
Lithuania	Vilnius	Lithuanian	Lithuanian	Lithuanians
Luxembourg	Luxembourg	French / German / Luxembourgish	Luxembourger	Luxembourgers
Malta	Valletta	Maltese / English	Maltese	Maltese
the Netherlands	Amsterdam	Dutch	Dutchman	Dutch
Poland	Warsaw	Polish	Pole	Poles
Portugal	Lisbon	Portuguese	Portuguese	Portuguese
Romania (Rumania / Roumania)	Bucharest	Rumanian	Romanian	Romanians
Slovenia	Ljubljana	Slovene	Slovene	Slovenes
Slovakia	Bratislava	Slovak	Slovak	Slovaks
Spain	Madrid	Spanish	Spaniard	Spanish
Sweden	Stockholm	Swedish	Swede	Swedes
the UK	London	English	Briton	Britons / British

Les faux amis

(False cognates)

Anglais	Traduction en français	Ne pas traduire par	Qui se dit en anglais
to achieve	réaliser, mener à bien	achever	to finish, to complete
actual	réel, concret	actuel	current, today's
actually	en fait	actuellement	nowadays, today, these days, currently, at present
affluence	richesse	affluence	rush
agenda	l'ordre du jour (d'une réunion)	agenda	diary, appointment book
appointment (1)	rendez-vous, nomination	appointements	salary, wages
to attend	assister à	attendre	to wait for, to expect
to attire	habiller	attirer	to attract
audience	le public, l'assistance	audience	ratings (2)
balance	équilibre	une balance	scales
benefit	avantage, allocation	bénéfice	profit
bribe (3)	pot-de-vin	bribe	fragment of a conversation
caution	prudence	caution	guarantee
chance	hasard, risque	chance	luck
to charge	faire payer	charger	to load
check	contrôle	chèque	cheque
confidence (4)	(généralement) confiance	confidence (NB)	a secret
commodity	marchandise	commodité	convenience
copy	exemplaire	copie	reproduction, fake
corporation	compagnie, société	corporation	profession, corporate body
to deceive	tromper	décevoir	to disappoint
deception	tromperie, duperie	déception	disappointment
delay	retard	délai	time limit
to demand	exiger	demander	to ask for
dismissal	licenciement	démission	resignation
to dispose of	se débarrasser de	disposer de	to have
dispute	conflit	dispute	quarrel, argument
education	scolarité, études	éducation	family upbringing
engagement	rendez-vous (5), fiançailles	engagement	commitment
equipment	le matériel	équipement	facilities
eventually	finalement	éventuellement	possibly
expertise	compétence	expertise	expert's report
fabrication (6)	invention (mensonge)	fabrication	manufacturing
to fix	réparer	fixer	to set
formation	création, fondation	formation	training
furniture	le mobilier	fournitures	supplies
issue (7)	a) question, émission d'actions b) différend c) numéro d'un journal	issue	exit, solution, outcome
journey	voyage	journée	day
location	emplacement, localisation	location	rental
mark	trace, signe, cicatrice	marque commerciale	a) brand(produits manufacturés) b) make (automobiles)

Anglais	Traduction en français	Ne pas traduire par	Qui se dit en anglais
notice	avis, préavis	notice	note, instructions
patron	client	patron	boss
petrol	essence	pétrole	(crude) oil, petroleum
politics (8)	les sciences politiques, la profession	la politique (stratégie)	policy (9)
prejudice	préjugé	préjudice	loss, harm, damage, wrong
to prevent	empêcher	prévenir	to warn, to tell
prime (adj)	premier, primordial, principal	prime prime (en + du salaire) d'assurance	premium bonus
publicity	la publicité, le battage médiatique	publicité (commerciale)	advertising
refuse	déchets, ordures	refus	refusal
to regard	considérer	regarder	to look at
to rest	se reposer	rester	to stay
to resume	reprendre, continuer, poursuivre	résumer	to summarize, to sum up
to survey	examiner	surveiller	to supervise
to use	utiliser	user	to wear out
vacancy	poste à pourvoir, chambre libre	vacances	vacation (US) holiday (UK)
valid	valable	valide	fit, well , valid (for a license)

(1) *Mr Fox is to take up an appointment as a researcher with the Royal Society.*
(2) *CBS's ratings showed huge improvement over last year.*
(3) *He was investigated for receiving bribes.*
(4) *Confidence* : peut se traduire par une confidence, un secret.
(5) *He couldn't come due to a previous engagement.*
(6) *It is pure fabrication (pure invention).*
(7) a) *An issue of shares, money, stamps.*
b) *The question has now become a real issue between the 2 countries* (cause de désaccord).
c) *The issue of a newspaper is the version of it published on a particular day.*
(8) *To go into politics* (faire de la politique).
(9) *EU Common Foreign Security Policy* (la politique étrangère et de sécurité commune de l'UE).
Policy : police d'assurance (dans l'assurance).

Les erreurs les plus fréquentes

(Common mistakes)

Type d'erreur	Ce qu'il faudrait écrire
Présent simple **(E)S** à la 3° pers. sing	+ : B.Verb. à ttes les pers. sauf **(E)S** à la 3e pers. sing.
	?/- : DO(NOT) ou DOES(NOT) + B.V.
Présent continu	+ : AM/ARE/IS + V. + ING ?/-: AM/ARE/IS (NOT)+ V. + ING
Preterit simple	+ : V + ED ou forme irrég. à ttes les pers. ?/-: DID NOT + **B.V.** à ttes les pers.
Present Perfect	+ : HAVE ou HAS + V.ED ?/- : HAVE ou HAS NOT + V.ED
Action Future	+ : WILL +B.V. à ttes les pers. ?/- : WILL NOT / WON'T + B.V.
Conditionnel	+ : WOULD + B.V. à ttes les pers. ?/-: WOULD NOT + B.V.
CAN / MUST/ SHOULD...	AUX. + **B.V.**
Forme négative (absence d'auxil., place négation)	voir les temps concernés
Forme interrogative	voir les temps concernés
The / A / An / Ø	the : le, la, les a/an : un, une Ø : des, du, de la / le, la, les suivant les cas
Accord déterm. / nom/ verbe	sujet et verbe ou auxiliaire au même genre déterminant et nom au même genre
Some / Any / No	some : du, de, le, des (phrase affirmative any : du, de, le, des (phrase interrogative ou négative) no : pas de (phrase de sens négatif)
Pronoms personnels sujets	I, you, he, she, it, we, you, they
Pronoms personnels compléments	Me, you, him, her, it, us, you, them
Adjectifs possessifs	my, your, his, her, its, our, your, their
Pronoms possessifs	mine, yours, his, hers, its, ours, yours, theirs
Cas possessif	It's Paul' sweater
Adjectifs	se place **devant** le nom est invariable, **pas de S au pluriel**.
Adjectifs : comparatif et superlatif	More / adjectif + er /less... plus.../ moins ...que The most... / the least ... le plus... / le moins...
Adverbes : adjectif + ly	He looked at the car carefully.
Who / Which / That What / Whose	who : pour une personne which : chose ou animal that : pour les deux cas whose : dont what : ce que , ce qui
Who ? What ? How + adjectif ...?	Who are you ? How old are you ?
Pour traduire « POUR »	Pour + verbe : **TO + B.V.** Pour + nom : **FOR + nom**
Je suis d'accord avec Je ne suis pas d'accord avec	I agree with... I do not agree / I disagree with...

Les fautes d'orthographe à éviter

(Spelling mistakes)

Certains mots sont souvent mal orthographiés par contagion avec le français.

- **Exemple**

environment

Erreurs fréquentes	Orthographe correcte
accomodation	accommodation
adress	address
agressive	aggressive
an other	another
are'nt	aren't
can not	cannot
comparaison	comparison
competitivness	competitiveness
dispite	despite
developped	developed
environnement	environment
exemple	example
exercice	exercise
familly	family
governement	government
immediatly	immediately
inacceptable	unacceptable
independance	independence
is'nt	isn't
negociation	negotiation
occurence	occurrence
prefered	preferred
rationnal	rational
responsability	responsibility
standart	standard
traditionnal	traditional

L'anglais britannique et l'anglais américain

(British English and American English)

▸ Différences lexicales

Certains mots sont différents en Grande-Bretagne et aux États-Unis.

British English	American English	French
autumn	fall	automne
bill	check	addition (restaurant)
biscuit	cookie	gâteau sec
bonnet	hood	capot de voiture
boot	trunk	coffre de voiture
car park	parking lot	parking
chemist's	drugstore	pharmacie
chips	French fries	frites
cinema, pictures	movie	cinéma
engaged	busy	occupé (ligne téléphonique)
film	movie	film
fireman	fire-fighter	pompier
flat	apartment	appartement
floor	storey	étage
form	class	classe
garden	yard	jardin
ground floor	first storey	rez-de-chaussée
handbag	purse	sac à main
holiday	vacation	vacances
hover	vacuum cleaner	aspirateur
jumper	sweater	pull over
junction	intersection	croisement
letter box	mail box	boîte à lettres
lift	elevator	ascenseur
lorry	truck	camion
motorway	freeway	autoroute
number plate	licence plate	plaque d'immatriculation
off-licence	liquor store	magasin de vins et spiritueux
paperback	pocket book	livre de poche
pavement	sidewalk	trottoir
petrol	gas	essence
postcode	zip code	code postal
postman	mail carrier	facteur
queue	line	file d'attente
rubber	eraser	gomme
rubbish	trash, garbage	ordures
shop	store	magasin
shop assistant	clerk	vendeur
sweets	candy	bonbons
tap	faucet	robinet
tin	can	boîte de conserve
toilet	restroom	toilettes
trousers	pants	pantalon
underground	subway	métro

▸ Différences othographiques

Certains mots ont une orthographe différente en Grande-Bretagne et aux États-Unis.

British spelling	American spelling
catalogue centre a cheque a defence a grey jacket an honour labour levelled out three metres neighbour to organise a plough a programme quarelling subsidise totalling travelling	catalog center a check defense a gray jacket an honor labor leveled out three meters neighbor to organize a plow a program quarreling subsidize totaling traveling

En général on peut constater que :

	British spelling	American spelling
la finale « tre » →« ter »	theatre	theater
la finale « our » → « or »	colour	color
la finale « ise » → « ize »	realise	realize
le « l » final n'est pas doublé	travelled	traveled
la finale « ence » → « ense »	licence	license

▸ Différences phonologiques

Quelques exemples parmi d'autres à découvrir :

Les consonnes	
British	**American**
/t/	/d/ atténué
thirty / letter / later	
la lettre» r» →/ ə /	la lettre» r» →/r/
letter / later	

Les voyelles	
British	**American**
/ɔː/	/ɑː/
ball / caught	
/ɑː/	/æ/
can't / fast / class	

▸ Grammaire

Trois différences importantes au niveau des verbes :

• utilisation du prétérit au lieu du present perfect pour exprimer un bilan avec « just » (Ex : I just came back from the USA.) ;

• emploi très restreint de « have got » ;
• certains verbes irréguliers :
– certains verbes irréguliers en anglais sont réguliers en américain ;

• **Exemple**
to burn / to dream / to learn...

– certains verbes réguliers en anglais sont irréguliers en américain.

• **Exemple**
to dive / to fit / to quit...

De plus, l'américain emploie parfois des prépositions différentes pour introduire les compléments de certains verbes :

British English	American English
Would you like to come and visit us? She wants to stay at home tonight.	Would you like to come and visit with us? She wants to stay home tonight.

La presse britannique et américaine

(British and American press)

▸ La presse britannique

Il existe deux formats de journaux :
- *broadsheet* (ou grand format) : ils sont associés à la presse de qualité (*Quality papers*) ;
- *tabloids* (ou presse à sensation).

La presse du dimanche :
- des journaux paraissant uniquement le dimanche ;
- des éditions du dimanche des quotidiens.

• Quality papers

The Daily Telegraph
http://www.telegraph.co.uk/
The Guardian
http://www.guardian.co.uk/
The Independent
http://www.independent.co.uk/
The Times
http://www.timesonline.co.uk/tol/news/
The Financial Times
http://www.ft.com/home/europe

• Sunday papers

The Observer
http://observer.guardian.co.uk/
The Sunday Times
http://www.timesonline.co.uk/tol/news/
The Independent on Sunday
http://www.independent.co.uk/
The Sunday Telegraph
http://www.telegraph.co.uk/
The News of the World
http://www.newsoftheworld.co.uk/

• Magazines

The Economist
http://www.economist.com/

▸ La presse américaine

• Quality papers

The Washington Post
http://www.washingtonpost.com/
The New York Times
http://www.nytimes.com/
USA Today
http://www.usatoday.com/
The International Herald Tribune (for expatriates)
http://www.iht.com/

• Magazines

Time
http://www.time.com/time/

Newsweek
http://www.newsweek.com/
Business Week
http://www.businessweek.com/
Fortune
http://money.cnn.com/magazines/fortune/

Crédits photographiques

p. 8	ph © Franco Vogt/Corbis
p. 70	© www.CartoonStock.com
p. 103	ph © Bob Englehart
p. 108	ph © Thomas Frey/dpa/Corbis
p. 114	ph © Fanny Tondre/REA
p. 144	© www.CartoonStock.com

Mise en page : STDI

Éditions Foucher 58, rue Jean-Bleuzen, 92178 Vanves Cedex –
Juin 2010 – 01 – MV-NG-CK/EP

Normandie Roto Impression s.a.s., 61250 Lonrai – N° d'impression : 102121 – Imprimé en France

IMPRIM'VERT